D1826021

Hi There, How Do I Know You?

Brandon D. Emery

Paperback ISBN: 978-1-64718-400-1
Hardcover ISBN: 978-1-64718-401-8

Published by BookLocker.com, Inc., St. Petersburg, Florida.

Printed on acid-free paper.

BookLocker.com, Inc.
2020

First Edition

Library of Congress Cataloging in Publication Data
Emery, Brandon D.
Hi There, How Do I Know You? by Brandon D. Emery
Library of Congress Control Number: 2020905171

Acknowledgments

For my wife Amanda and me, the creation of this book is our love story unfolding for the world to finally hear of God's remarkable plan that changed our lives forever. Without a doubt, my parents, Don and Becky Emery, played a vital role in helping the promise come to fruition. They both walk in prophetic realms, and are well respected in their accuracy with foretold events. They are senior pastors at our home church, Rugged Cross Chapel, which sits in the heart of southern Illinois. With over twenty years of ministerial experience, their presence in our lives is priceless. Being connected to God, they always knew the promise would take place, and had zero hesitation in our journey.

To my mom, thanks for keeping a calendar of everything that happens with our family. All the dates listed in this book come from your handwritten calendar! You are truly a wonderful mother. To my dad, you're my best friend. Pastor Don and Becky are true treasures, and for those who know them, count yourself blessed. For their unwavering faith, we respect and honor them publicly. I have watched them endure many things over the years, and not once did they not persevere with God to make it over the mountain. They are strong, fearless, and passionate about their servanthood to God. He has big plans in store for them as they press toward their destiny. We truly believe and know that the best is yet to be.

To all our friends and family, we love you. We could continually write on your important roles in our lives. You all hold a special place in our hearts. To Amanda's parents, Mike and Gayle Gill, your love and support have always been constant since the beginning. You have worked hard your whole lives to provide and bless your family. Thanks for everything that you do for us and the entire Gill household. To Micah and your beautiful kiddos, Jaxson and Delaney, you are simply the best. Your faith is a light to a fallen world. Continue to press on with God for without a doubt, He has great things in store. To Gabriel, you're an amazing brother. Thanks for all the laughs and fun times. Such good memories, and we thank God for you.

To Mark and Shannon and their lovely kiddos, Braden and Aleah, thanks for being there all these years. You are truly consistent in your walk with God, in season and out of season. We believe God will continually lift you higher and higher as you press toward your destiny. To Saundra, you're an incredible friend and thanks for everything. From our engagement photos at Bacon Creek to making blankets for all our children, you are a wonderful example of a true friend. To all our friends at Cornerstone World Outreach, we appreciate everything you have done for us. Thanks for lighting the path for Amanda to grow into a godly woman.

To our home church congregation at Rugged Cross Chapel, we thank the Lord for such a wonderful group of battle-tested believers. We fight the good fight of faith with you, and know God will use us to fulfill His perfect will in the days ahead. You all deserve much recognition. To know all of you, we consider ourselves blessed beyond measure. All the memories that we have created with friends and family will forever be etched in our hearts. The list could continue page after page of all the inspirational people in our lives, and we cannot wait to see what God is going to do in the years to come. As we pilgrim through this world in high expectation of our eternal heavenly home, we press toward the mark with all of you.

I personally want to mention my lovely wife, Amanda. She is indeed the apple of my eye, and I love enjoying life with her each and every day. In my eyes, she is the most beautiful woman who has ever walked this earth. Amanda is a joy to be around, loves God with all her heart, and makes every day special. She is indeed my better half, and as our family continues to grow, I strive to show her how much I love her. In addition, she is a fantastic mother! Having our three little blessings is such a joy in this life. With teething, diaper changes, bottles, hiccups, potty training, and little sleep, working tirelessly to write the book became a challenge. Amanda is a superstar mommy and rocked it out with class! She watched the kiddos while I worked on the book in our bedroom. We would do six-hour shifts on my days off for me to write, then I would take time to spend with the family.

All the moms out there know the feeling! Late at night, Amanda would read through the chapters to proofread for me, give critical feedback, and provide fresh ideas on things that happened from her perspective. With my work schedule, being an assistant pastor and raising a family, writing while being completely exhausted became a common theme. We would not trade our lives for the world, though, and when God wanted the book written quickly, we had to really push forward. With a newborn, a one-year-old, and a two-year-old, our book writing journey did not lack entertainment!

> "Happy is the man that hath his quiver
> full of them: they shall not be ashamed,
> but they shall speak with the enemies in
> the gate." – Psalms 127:5

As our lifelong adventure continues, I thank God for all He has done. Amanda is an amazing woman, and I consider myself highly blessed. Being orchestrated by God, she moved from Iowa to southern Illinois to start her life with me. Amanda is a great woman of faith, and God is going to take her into deeper spiritual levels with Him. I love you, Amanda.

And finally, without further ado, we give an enormous shout-out to our Lord and Savior, Jesus

Christ. He is truly the mastermind behind our relationship and deserves all the credit. Words do not express our allegiance to Him. We love Him above all else. He is truly the King of kings, and He does bless those who are called according to His purpose. He also is a God of communication, and knows how to lead His sheep. God led Amanda and me to one another through detailed prophecies, visions, and personal words. We know, without a doubt, He desires to let Christians know what His divine will is for their lives. He does not look at one's economic status, accomplishments, educational background, or any other characteristics that sets one apart through worldly means. Instead, He looks at the heart and examines one's intentions, obedience, faith, and willingness to follow Him. Let His mighty name be glorified throughout all generations for being such an impartial God. Believe me, if He can do this mighty love matching thing for a country boy from the backwoods of southern Illinois, He can do it for anyone. The Bible states His impartiality perfectly:

> "For there is no respect of persons with God." – Romans 2:11

Earthly words do not convey how amazing God is, but throughout this book, we do our best to highlight His glorious presence in our lives. We testify of His greatness, and thank Him for everything good that He has graciously bestowed on us. He is not some being in the sky that we never hear from, but instead, a Father who cares about us. Whether sitting in a lawn chair, walking through a mall, or driving down a gravel road,

God is always there. In this life, we do not understand everything that happens, but one constant assurance remains: God has it all figured out. I quoted the Scripture below countless times while waiting for Amanda, and even though I did not understand everything, I knew God loved me, communicated with me, and had my life figured out to fulfill His will.

> "For I know the thoughts that I think toward you, saith the Lord, thoughts of peace, and not of evil, to give you an expected end." – Jeremiah 29:11

Table of Contents

Introduction

We have written this book to share our love story with you, and to acknowledge how great our God is, for without Him, Amanda and I would have never met. In a fallen world filled with chaos and trouble, God is still number one with relationships, marriage, and family. Raised a country boy, who greatly values privacy, I now open up about my life to help Christians see how God operates. With all the filth in romantic books and movies today, our love story offers the world a clean alternative to romance. There are many ways in which couples meet, but in our journey, God truly acted as the matchmaker.

To walk in complete faith and obedience takes guts, and it is not for the faint of heart. We read about all the glorious testimonies throughout the Bible because faithful believers never quit on what God told them. Their stories are included in the bestselling book of all time due to their ferocious determination to finish their course. And thousands of years later, Amanda and I are writing our own testimony. This book may not be the most polished, but it is one of the most genuine books one will ever read. I am certainly not a seasoned writer, but my main purpose for the creation of this book is focused on helping young people do things the right way with God. Up to this point, this is the only book I have ever written, and I believe it will help teenagers and young adults from all walks of life.

Learning how God works according to His Word changes the lens by which we view this world. His presence can burn mountains and simultaneously melt hearts with a pure and genuine love. So many people go through life looking for something to fill the void inside them. If they would simply give their life over to Christ, He could lead them into realms they never thought possible. The Christian life, if done correctly, is the most exciting and rewarding journey that one can experience in this world. Everything else isn't even a distant second!

Beginning with day one of our initial contact, Amanda and I always felt like we were in a dream. God had finally done what He had said, and it became surreal as we lived the promise. When God turned the captivity of Zion in Psalm 126, they said, "We were like them that dream." This chapter always burns inside of me because with God, supernatural blessings do happen. As prophecy unfolded before our very eyes, much like Israel, we had to pinch ourselves to make sure we were not dreaming. This is how Amanda and I felt as we progressed through the different stages of our relationship with one another. We were living a life that God had created for us, and with every day that went by, we fell deeper in love. All the first-time stuff gave me goosebumps! Hearing Amanda's voice for the first time, receiving my first handwritten letter, holding her hand for the first time, attending our first church service together, and all the special "firsts" in between made the love journey breathtaking. God can supernaturally put couples together for those who know His voice, strictly obey His commands, and do His will. We are living testimonies of God orchestrating a divine relationship!

> "And the Lord God said, it is not good
> that the man should be alone; I will make
> him a help meet for him" – Genesis 2:18

No one understands romance like God. He knew exactly what He had planned for Amanda and me, and He perfectly mixed love with His divine will. With dating websites, online compatibility tests, blind date hookups, self-help books, etcetera, it makes sense to just rely on the best matchmaker of all time. This is exactly what I did in my journey and it really works! I fixed my mind on God and followed Him. If He could speak to Elijah in a still small voice, speak to Moses through a burning bush, and speak through a donkey to Balaam, then surely God could speak to me in this present world. With all the things God is capable of, I just gave Him complete control of my life, and this included my relationships.

Oftentimes, church people are silent on romance, marital sex, and passionate love, but God is the one who created it all. Christian couples should have the best relationships this world has ever seen. Why? Christ is first and the relationship is governed by Him. This does not mean it is a perfect world of harmony, though, because unique personalities, love languages, interests, stress factors, ways of coping, living habits, emotions, ways of communication, etcetera, make married life a constant work in progress. But indeed, the benefits of a God-centered marriage far outweigh the challenges of growing old as a couple.

To our readers, have hope in God! Build yourself up in His Word and believe His promises. If He can do a miracle for us, He can surely do one for you! Am I suggesting that God will move the exact same way in your life as He did in ours? Of course not, but He may do something similar, or He may do things totally different in your story. We have learned to not put God in a box. He is a creator by nature so we just let Him do what He does best. What can you do as a single Christian man or woman? Begin positioning yourself today for His bountiful blessings, and live as the infallible Word states. Do what He says to do, resist the devil, flee from temptation, and walk like a soldier in the greatest army to ever exist.

The Christian life is not always easy, but oh my, it sure is worth it. God is the "X" factor, and with Him, you should like your odds of being successful in this fallen world. If God can catch Elijah up in a chariot of fire, use Moses to part the Red Sea, birth the Savior of the world from a virgin woman, make the sun stand still for Joshua, and connect Amanda and me who lived states away, He can do mighty things in your life as well.

You have one lifelong opportunity to leave a legacy behind, and truly obtain what God has for you. Bust through mediocre living and thrive in living victoriously. We read about all the great stories in the Bible about men and women who stretched their faith to succeed with God. If you do it God's way, you can conquer mountains and invade the territory of the devil. Do the impossible and forget about anything that is contrary to the Word of God. In the ministry of Jesus, He released a faith bomb in reference to a rich man entering the Kingdom of Heaven:

> "But Jesus beheld them, and said unto them, with men this is impossible; but with God all things are possible."
> – Matthew 19:26

I view life much like this as well. If things line up with God's will, just like personal salvation, then do the impossible and break through! Do not be lazy or fearful, go conquer what God says you can obtain in His Word. One cannot be a couch potato and expect great things to just randomly happen. God rewards those who do His will. This means attending a "biblically sound" church, establishing a prayer life, remaining out of sinful pleasures, seeking the baptism of the Holy Ghost, learning God's voice for yourself, paying tithes and offerings, and working within your local church to build His Kingdom. As Christians, we cannot expect God to bless us if we do not do things His way. With God, it's His way or the highway. So many think they can just bargain with God or push Him to do things their way. He is King, though! It's a great benefit to us if we simply listen and obey! Besides, He knows more about life than we do, and like any good father, He has our best interest in mind.

Amanda and I always knew we would be writing this book. I can recall telling Amanda on the first day we met in person that we would write a book on this someday. Throughout the bigger-than-life moments, I strategically jotted things down so I could precisely tell our love story. We actually thought it would be soon after our wedding, but we had to wait for God's timing. I stood before everyone at our wedding reception, grabbed the microphone, and told them all to look for our book one day. I could not wait to share one of the best love stories ever told. In fact, having been in church since the young age of five, I have never heard anything like it. Our journey is special, and we will use our testimony to shine the spotlight on Christ. He deserves all the credit and recognition!

Amanda and I have been happily married for four years now, and time continues to fly by. My priorities simply turned upside down one morning in the summer of year 2019; as I stepped out of bed, God placed in my spirit to begin the assignment of writing our book. It burned like an ember in my heart, and it overtook my thoughts. My dad even confirmed it a few days later through prophecy. God told him for me to, "Write the book quickly." Immediately, I told Amanda that we didn't even have a computer for me to start, so we took a part of our savings to purchase a laptop. We installed a basic writing program on it, and being my first book, I just dove into it headfirst.

I felt like Peter when he decided to step out of the boat. I became fearlessly obedient and simply trusted God to do the rest! Most condemn Peter for faltering on the sea, but at least he had the guts to step out of the boat in the first place. He walked on water that night with Jesus while everyone else stayed in their comfort zone. To do great things in this life, I believe everyone needs a "step out in faith" moment to propel them into the unknown. Most people never change their life due to fear, and as a result, their adaptation to the circumstances freezes them in time. Be like Peter; step out onto the raging waters and experience breathtaking things. Your life can change for the better!

This book is a genuine faith booster! It is neither fiction nor a cookie-cutter story. These are real-life events that God orchestrated, and as I wrote our love story one page at a time, tears often came forth as I caught myself reminiscing over our amazing journey. We are super stoked to finally share our love story with you. Always count on God and never give up, for God is more than able to bring His promises to pass. In our experience, walking in obedience, standing strong in faith, and remaining out of sin are keys to unlocking God's great benefits that He stores up for the righteous. He does care about you, wants great relationships in your life, and paves the way for you to be victorious in these areas. Be blessed as your faith rises while you receive a firsthand encounter with how He works in this world. Do not let the ups and downs discourage you. Connect yourself with His will and fight to thrive in it. God knows all, sees all, and understands all. If you are honestly trying, He has you cradled in the palms of His mighty hands.

And if you are happily married, recommend this book for all the single gents and gals in your life. It can save them much misery and time if they do things right from the start with their preparation of marrying their lifelong companion. Having God as the matchmaker is a no-lose situation. If you're a parent or grandparent, purchase it for your children. It will be some of the best money you will ever spend. Years of our lives bottled up in an easy-to-read book that shows how God works in the lives of believers.

As the Bible clearly states, we acknowledge that our sworn enemy comes to steal, kill, and destroy. We understand that we must fight to win on each battlefield against the kingdom of darkness. Whether the battlefield is in the mind or in the physical, we are guaranteed victory through the power of the Word. Not sure about you, but most of the battles I have faced in my life have been between the inches of space between my ears. The mind is a war zone sometimes! Thoughts, dreams, demonic voices, and ungodly human voices constantly try to have rent-free status in our heads. But I testify, we can have a sound mind as the Bible tells us. Taking thoughts into captivity and anything that does not line up with the Word takes effort, but control your mind and everything else will follow.

I had to be proactive in controlling my mind while waiting for Amanda, and thanks be to God, who is far above any earthly counsellor. He knows us better than we know ourselves, so giving Him full control is a great idea. Letting Him just do His thing requires no fees or additional charges either. In my experiences, I know He loves counseling me on my level, and truly lives up to His name of being the "Wonderful Counselor." God built spiritual strongholds in my mind that the devil could not penetrate. Ministers often talk about tearing down strongholds, which is true, but establishing biblical fortifications in the mind helps quench all the fiery darts from our sworn enemy. Your mind is like a castle; defend it!

Humble Beginnings

Amanda and I lived nearly 650 miles apart, which is approximately a ten-hour driving distance, but God Himself arranged our marriage. Seem a bit far-fetched? Stay with me! I live in West Frankfort, a very small town on the southern tip of Illinois. Amanda lived in Sioux City, Iowa, which sits in a triangle of three states consisting of Iowa, Nebraska, and South Dakota. It wasn't like we could just meet each other for lunch or grab a latte after work. We had some serious distance between us that only God could manage. I had never been to Iowa, and Amanda had no aspirations to take up residence in southern Illinois. But little did we know, God would intersect our paths despite all the miles between us. Distance to Him is irrelevant, and He can connect people worldwide in a short amount of time. We discovered through our amazing journey that He is really good at Christian love stories.

We were united through prophecy alone! Over the years, I have seen prophecies happen that were foretold by my parents up to ten years in advance. It is common territory in my life. And with our love story, my parents and I received visions and words for almost four years about Amanda. The details in the words and visions are precise and accurate. For example, I knew Amanda's height and hair color years before we met, my mom knew her first name, and my dad knew I needed to open a Facebook account to kickstart our divine connection. Crossing state lines, we followed God to meet the woman I would indeed marry. We were married in ten months after our initial contact! Throughout the book, we use photos taken from our journey to further encapsulate God's divine plan. As our love story unfolds for you, let God be glorified.

On a military base in 1990, Amanda came into the world in Okinawa, Japan. Her father, Mike, served in the United States Marine Corps during this time as a canine instructor for the base. Amanda comes from a military family, and they have a deep love for this great country. Moving from one military base to the next, Amanda eventually landed in Sioux City, Iowa, with her family. I, on the other hand, came into this world in the middle of the United States in my current hometown of West Frankfort.

The town I grew up in is so small that if you blink, you might miss it while traveling down the interstate. Amanda grew up a city girl near the Iowa state line, and I grew up a country boy on a small farm out in the middle of nowhere. On our family farm, we had horses, rabbits, chickens, pigs, and goats. We put up barbed wire fences in the spring, baled hay in the summer, cut firewood in the fall, and bust ice for livestock to drink in the winter. I grew up fishing and hunting and spent much of my childhood in open fields and vast woodlands. The old country saying "Were you born in a barn?" fits my upbringing perfectly.

Living about forty-five minutes from the Kentucky border, my family knew how to survive off the land. I love the outdoors, and have a great appreciation for the beautiful landscapes God has given us. Amanda had a much different geographical upbringing, and lived much of her childhood primarily in cities. I always think in the theater of my mind that Amanda strolled malls as a teenager and hung out with friends at the movies, while I collected chicken eggs! She spent much time shopping with her sister Micah and enjoying all the activities in Omaha, Nebraska, which is just over an hour away from Sioux City. Being sisters, they share an inseparable bond, and still communicate on a daily basis.

For summer vacation time, Amanda always loved the trips to the country while visiting her grandma's farm in Colorado. They had cows, chickens, goats, horses, and farmland so she always loved the freedom away from city life. Amanda loved riding four-wheelers throughout the farm, playing with her grandma's rottweilers, and capturing photos of the Colorado sunsets just in sight over the cornfields. Good thing! God knew the whole time that she would eventually marry a pastor who is a bona fide country boy.

Now that we live outside of city limits, Amanda loves country life more than ever. We love the privacy, the nature around us, and the stillness, which helps time slow down. In the book of Matthew, we find Jesus disappearing as well to be alone.

> "And when he had sent the multitudes away, he went up into a mountain apart to pray: and when the evening was come, he was there alone." – Matthew 14:23

I have always loved how Jesus himself took time away from the crowds to pray. For us, living in the country is a quiet place where we can rest in God. We can simply walk outside and be alone with Him. Whether praying under the stars, in the barn on a rainy day, or when the sun gleams down, having the alone time puts our focus on Him. It is such an important thing to make time for God. In the rat race society that we live in, constant prioritizing has to be in place. For if one is too busy for God, then they are just simply not obeying His Word.

In my earlier years, I built a treehouse next to a five-acre fescue field. I remember my dad always telling me when I looked bored to go lay in my treehouse and spend time in prayer. In that old tree house, I began establishing my relationship with God, and as an adult, I love being with God in still moments. Amanda always loved praying in the outdoors as well, and often went to a hill next to her childhood church. She would pray to God as the wind whipped on top of that hill, and oh my, God surely heard her prayers. It is a common similarity between us that we both ran to the outdoors to pray. This morning, before writing this segment, Amanda went on a jog down our country road to spend time with her Savior. There is just something special about spending time with God as Adam and Eve did in the beginning. They walked with God in the cool of the day, and developed their relationship with Him through communication. God loves to talk about every aspect of our lives. He craves conversations with us, and created mankind to have close fellowship with Him. So, instead of texting and dialing numbers all the time, we should start conversations with the God of the universe!

We definitely came from different upbringings, but a common similarity emerged: we both loved God with all our hearts. Even as kids, we had such a desire to please Him in any capacity to help be a light in a dark world. It's amazing to look at the roadways in which life took us, and years later, God intersecting our paths. One of Amanda's paths involved serving nine years in the Air National Guard. Amanda has flown many times in planes within the states and abroad. She has crossed oceans, been on foreign lands, and even won the national John L. Hennessy Award for her military service. I on the other hand, have never seen an ocean, never flown in a plane, and only been to a handful of states! I attended a local university and received my master's degree in education. In the physical realm, I have lived a pretty average life compared to some. But not Amanda!

It's funny because when we go out to eat on Veterans Day, I usually ask the server, "Do you give a military discount?" They usually immediately start thanking me for my service, but I have to quickly inform them that Amanda is the military vet! I am like, "Yeah, my wife is one tough cookie!" Amanda followed her dad's footsteps and loved the military, but she began to feel by God that she would be exiting at some point. She had enlisted for another two years in year 2014, but as God kept nudging her, she knew her time in the Air Guard would be coming to an end. She had no idea why God continued to lead her this way, but we eventually found out His reasoning. Like a giant chessboard, God began to position her to be married. He also knew that she would be moving to a different state, and would no longer be able to work at her current base.

God is huge on alignment! Years in advance, He began lining things up to fulfill His plan. He loved Amanda enough to let her know things would be changing. Just by that little nudge, she knew He definitely had a plan. Around the same time frame, she became a secretary at her church. Working with pastors on a daily basis gave her first-hand experience of what it is like to be in the full-time ministry. Being she would marry a pastor, God positioned Amanda to be ready not only for a husband, but to be an integral part of our ministry in southern Illinois.

Always remember, God is years ahead of the physical realm in which we live. Even if something does not make sense, obey Him! He often moves His children like pawns on a chessboard to pave the way for His perfect will. Many people miss opportunities with God because they try to reason everything out and determine whether or not it makes sense to them. But if one truly knows God's voice, they must simultaneously understand that His ways are above ours. God sees days, months, and years into the future. If we truly trust Him, and believe He directs our footsteps, then we must move quickly even though it makes no sense. In doing so, we must first understand that God will never contradict His Word. This simple truth is a big part of the litmus test. If one ever thinks they are hearing from God, but it does not line up with Scripture, then they are listening to their own thoughts or a demon. Knowing the voice of God is imperative to following Him. I cannot stress this powerful truth enough.

> "And when he putteth forth his own sheep, he goeth before them, and the sheep follow him: for they know his

voice. And a stranger will they not follow, but will flee from him: for they know not the voice of strangers." – John 10:4-5

You first have to be of the sheepfold, and secondly, you have to know the Shepherd's voice. For an illustration, my sister used to call home, and I pretended to be my dad when I answered. I tried to fool her, but she instantly knew that I was not him. Even though I could fool many who called, she had spent too much time with her father. It is the same with our heavenly Father. If one spends enough time with Him, they will learn to distinguish and harken to His voice. And with other voices, they will quickly dismiss. Devils love to mimic God's voice so learning "what is not God" is just as important as learning the voice of our Shepherd. With knowing how to follow God, in the valleys and on the mountaintops, one is light years away from this world in terms of having a divine connection that will lead them to a better place. If you personally want God to lead you to green pastures and still waters metaphorically speaking, you better take time to truly know His voice. Being connected to God is the number one thing in this dramatic love story that led my parents and I to Sioux City, Iowa. In the book of Psalms, David the poet testifies of how God truly does lead.

"He maketh me to lie down in green pastures: he leadeth me beside the still waters. He restoreth my soul: he leadeth me in the paths of righteousness for his

name's sake. Yea, though I walk through
the valley of the shadow of death, I will
fear no evil: for thou art with me; thy rod
and thy staff they comfort me." – Psalms
23:2-4

Amanda and I both shared a fierce commitment to
obeying God from a very young age. As the old saying
goes, "Obedience is easy, but disobedience is very
difficult." We always strived to obey God to the best of
our abilities. We were taught correctly in that blessings
pursue the obedient, and judgment awaits the
disobedient. Just like the law of gravity, it is what it is.
Those who are wise just submit to this divine principle.
We are so thankful to our parents for taking us to church
when we were young. Attending Sunday school,
memorizing Scripture, learning to pray, singing "Jesus
Loves Me," blessing our food, and doing biblical things
are deeply embedded in both of our childhoods. Our
parents dressed us on Sunday mornings, fed us
breakfast, and made sure we were at church to learn and
worship. It is hands down the greatest gift that a child
can receive.

Over the years, being taken to God's house to not
only learn the Word, but to build our personal
relationship with Him, propelled us in our spiritual
walks. Many young people unfortunately leave church
in early adulthood because they never experience a
personal relationship with Jesus Christ nor see anything
happen spiritually. As humans, we need to experience
the presence of God! Church is boring and redundant if

we never experience the supernatural side of God. For example, being baptized in the Holy Ghost at a youth back-to-school retreat in my early teen years, with the evidence of speaking in unknown tongues, I knew the Book of Acts pertained to my life. When supernatural things written in the Scriptures happen in one's life, such as talking in their Heavenly language, it is captivating. The Word mixed with spiritual power creates a dynamic duo that can be seen, felt, and heard.

When Amanda and I first started communicating, I stood in awe of her knowledge of the Word, and how close to God she walked. Amanda is definitely a woman of faith, and she is fierce when it comes to trusting God. She knows parts of the Old Testament better than I do, and I admire her walk with God. Learning that grace is not a license to sin, knowing how to resist temptations, submitting to godly authority, paying tithes and offerings, attending God's house on a consistent basis, praying in the Holy Ghost, and memorizing Scripture are all just tipping the iceberg for all she learned through those critical years of a young lady. Amanda has always stayed with God, and Scripture rings true as she continues to draw closer to Him. This is one of the main reasons she never rebelled on God. She cannot fathom life without Him, and from a very young age, she became hardwired to never backslide.

> "Train up a child in the way he should go: and when he is old, he will not depart from it." – Proverbs 22:6

With me, my family started attending a local church around the same time I turned five years old. My dad always knew he had a divine calling to preach. To make a long story shorter, he ran from his calling in his early adult years, but after receiving life-threatening doctor reports, he completely decided to serve God all his days. Doctors gave him only six months to live, but due to his complete surrender to God, he received a radical healing. Doctors told him that no hope existed, and basically sent him home to live out his last days. In our small white farmhouse, we quickly learned that God had other plans!

My dad crawled on his hands and knees to our old horse barn to pray, and he knew it had to be God or he would die. In that barn, he laid on the dirt floor and cried out to God in complete desperation. My dad had a Holy Ghost-filled upbringing, and his grandparents were anointed preachers, so he knew how to get ahold of God. We didn't miss church either! I remember my dad leaning on my mom as she tried to help him to the car. My mom would drive the family to a small country church, and men would come out to carry my dad in the doors. Being weak and sick, they just laid him on the back pew. Through faith and obedience, he basically resurrected! That happened almost thirty years ago, and he has been preaching ever since. The devil tried his best to take him out early, but my dad kept fighting the good fight of faith. Come on now, God still heals!

A few years down the road, after God healed my dad, I spent much time traveling with my parents while ministering to churches. Under the wise counsel of our pastor, my dad followed God in being a guest speaker. We drove an old brown four-door car that did not start half the time. We kept a can of gas in the trunk to prime the engine! We would often park in the back of the parking lot to avoid the car dying on us in front of everyone. But one thing for sure, we always did our best to make God happy. My dad would preach Hell and brimstone as the old saying goes, and we saw God move in mighty ways. Before we arrived at the church, we would ask my dad, "Is it a fire burner?" If he responded "yes," this meant people were going to probably get mad! We would often tell my mom to start the car early so we could all jump into the car through the side door of the church. We were half serious and half joking!

During my childhood years, my family struggled with finances, and my parents would not eat on some occasions so my sister and I could. Many looked down on us due to the way we dressed, what we drove, and where we lived. The looks, the chuckles, and the whispers were a common occurrence. I found out quickly while growing up in church culture, there are many pastors or church leaders who only help those who benefit them personally. It's a shame, but often the poor family on the back pew receives the least amount of biblical help. They are not in the church "cliques," cannot drop a thousand dollars in the offering plate, and cannot volunteer every day because the parents work low-level jobs that require heavy hours. Throughout the ministry of Jesus, though, He treated the beggars and the rich folks equally.

Before our church services start now, I often head for the back rows for this reason. Whether one comes to church with a sports car, a jeep, a bicycle, or a mule, we should all strive to be like Christ. We should not embarrass people, should not look down our noses, but instead, wholeheartedly love our fellow brethren. Being on the road as a kid ministering with my family has served me well in my adult years. Being the kid on the back row gave me a lens to view things of what NOT to do. I understand that anointing or godliness is not determined by earthly possessions. We all came into this world the same way, and will all leave in much likeness.

> "For we brought nothing into this world,
> and it is certain we can carry nothing out.
> And having food and raiment let us be
> therewith content." – I Timothy 6:7-8

As my childhood went by, my dad received a direct command from God to start a church. We birthed out a full gospel ministry in West Frankfort, Illinois. After much prayer and a biblical release from our home church in year 2000, we began Rugged Cross Chapel. I had just turned thirteen years old when we began our family ministry. Our first service began in the town park with just my parents plus my sister and me. Being so young, I remember sitting at the picnic table and asking my dad if I could go chase squirrels. He responded with a sharp no, and from that day forward, we even had to wear church clothes to the park! We moved to our first building in the year 2001 and have not looked back since. Now in our second building, we still preach the Word faithfully every week. Our secret place is our church, and we strive to make it a safe haven for disciples of Christ. Thank the Lord that we still live in a country where we can assemble ourselves together for church freely without breaking any laws.

With me, I always knew God had a calling on my life to preach. A true prophetess who my family respected greatly, who has since gone home to be with the Lord, prophesied over me many years ago that I would pick up the Bible and begin to teach the Word. This lady came from the hills of Arkansas, small in stature, but moved in great Holy Ghost power. She is one of the most influential people that I have ever had the pleasure of knowing. With her confirming what I already knew, I took joy in knowing God had a big plan for my life as a preacher. With the Holy Ghost, I stepped behind the pulpit with a burning desire to teach the Word. With everything God had done for me over the course of many years, serving Him became my reasonable service.

Even now, put me in a small group or large crowd and I will be trying to preach to someone. I think all true ministers filled with the Holy Ghost share this same burning desire. Its life-changing, and dictates how we live life. I have been preaching over ten years now almost every Sunday. The pulpit area is my happy place, and even though it brings me out of my comfort zone, I know God is well pleased. There is something special about going to bed at night knowing I am right with God. To lay my head on a pillow with a clear conscience puts me at ease. I know whatever happens in this life, I am on my way to Heaven.

As of today, I am the assistant pastor of our ministry, and Amanda works heavily in our praise and worship. Together, we strive to glorify God, and show our appreciation to our Lord who uses the earth as His footstool. With my family, we preach the Word in season and out of season without compromising its integrity. In a fallen and dark society, the Bible is the moral compass of the world, and we press toward sharing its remarkable truths. I ran into our former pastor recently, and he asked if I still ministered. I said, "Yes, every Sunday," and he shook his fist in excitement. To see a child from his Sunday school program emerge into a preacher has to be a great reward.

Now in my early thirties, I have never quit on God because I am convinced without a doubt that He is Lord of all. I encourage every parent and grandparent to take their children to Sunday school in a church that resembles the ones in the Book of Acts. Let it have sound doctrine, power, and consistency. It is an early steppingstone for children to connect with the living God, and ultimately, the hope of America. The moral decay happening right now is a direct result of God's laws being severely disobeyed. The hope of this country is the one who sits on the Heavenly throne. Obey Him alone, and everything else will begin to reap the benefits of godly living. His ways are the greatest for any person, family, or society.

As a preacher kid, I constantly found myself under the microscope of everyone in and out of church. The standard is high for preacher kids, and my sister Shannon described it perfectly in a sermon once, in that it feels like we are in a giant goldfish bowl. Everyone who comes by the bowl looks and observes us, then goes about their daily routine. All the scrutiny, unrealistic expectations, and cruel treatment from so-called "church folk" can be a trap to push preacher kids away from God. People often said we would rebel on God eventually, since the statistics of quitting church upon adulthood is high for preacher kids. But Shannon and I never left church because we were taught how to connect with God on a personal level.

Growing up in church, I honestly never enjoyed the thought of being a preacher. Having witnessed firsthand how people treated my parents over the years, I did not want to continue in that lifestyle. But as of today, I am an assistant pastor! Been preaching for several years now, and I do my best for God, day in and day out. For me, no matter the pressure, Christ is worth living for all my days. Until I take my last breath on this earth, I will spread the glorious gospel.

We stay upbeat as a church family, confident in our Lord, but this does not mean we do not go through things in this fallen world. Often, our faith is stretched, and we have to pull deep from the living well inside of us to continue forward with God. Temptations, tribulations, demonic attacks, and dealing with ungodly people keep us on our knees praying. According to Scripture, we are not supposed to think of ourselves more highly than we should. If Christ suffered for well doing, then as His followers, we must expect the same. We also know that without Christ, we have no hope or future.

God compares humans to sheep, which are not the smartest animals in the barnyard. We become wise when we distinguish how frail we are in the grand scheme of things. I have personally been through many things in my life, and within this book, I will cast light onto those dark shadows. I have never cussed, never drank, never done drugs, never smoked or chewed, never quit church, remained faithful, etcetera, but in this next chapter, I will highlight the dark days that God carried me through, and tell you how I survived.

Dark Days

Married young at the age of twenty-one, I became divorced almost three years later in July 2011. Within this chapter, I talk about the dark time in my life, but have no contempt toward any parties involved. According to Scripture, God hath called us to forgiveness and peace, which I have been taught in church since my youth. This life-altering event spiraled me into an unknown darkness that I had never experienced before in my life. A darkness that few understand unless they have walked in those shoes. The dark days tested my inner man at such a level, it shook me to my core.

As I attempt to put words on paper, it is hard to convey the helplessness that I felt during those days. Being saved at the age of five in a small country church, I experienced the mighty presence of God. We rarely missed a service, and even though we were poor, our dedication to God never wavered. I can remember running squirrels out of that one-room building, using an outhouse due to no indoor plumbing, and hearing the floors creak as I walked across them, but wow, the anointing of God gust through that place. I feared God in a good way, and greatly desired to obey His Word.

I never in a million years thought I would be divorced, and had so many struggles that only God could carry me through. I understood that God utterly hates divorce, and I struggled greatly with this obvious truth many nights. Christians are supposed to be married one time in their life, not seek other relationships or sexual satisfactions, and not use divorce as a way to run from trouble. The core values of marriage are ordained by God, and within the marital covenant, the man and woman should please God according to His governing laws. For starters, we read in Ephesians that husbands should love their wives as Christ did the church, and wives in return should submit to their husbands. This order in the marriage is well pleasing unto God.

> "Wives, submit yourselves unto your own husbands, as unto the Lord. For the husband is the head of the wife, even as Christ is the head of the church: and he is the savior of the body. Therefore, as the church is subject unto Christ, so let the wives be to their own husbands in everything. Husbands, love your wives, even as Christ also loved the church, and gave himself for it." – Ephesians 5:22-25

As we read in context, we see that Christ died for the church, and men should esteem their wives in such a way. Likewise, women should submit to their husbands as the church does to Christ. This is just the beginning of what is required by both parties, but clearly, God created boundaries and criteria for a godly marriage. My parents will be married forty years this year, and are a great reflection of how a Christian marriage should operate. Through the years, they have remained committed despite all the odds stacked against them. But with me, I experienced a much different road. A road that I did not see coming, but one that I found myself on before my last semester of graduate school.

In the days following the divorce, thoughts of suicide, thoughts of inadequacy, thoughts of my life being over, thoughts of failing God, and severe depression emerged as the immediate threats to my well-being. It's tough lying awake at night with demons speaking lies of suicide. It's extremely difficult to walk in faith as ungodly people laugh from a distance. It's hard to cope with a whirlwind of emotions, feelings, and thoughts while still being in shock. But within the darkness, my glimmer of hope rested on the rock, Jesus Christ.

To be at the bottom of the barrel, so to speak, I had to climb out of the darkness one day at a time. Over the next several months, I defeated thoughts, emotions, and fiery darts from the wicked one on a regular basis. Many nights, I would lay awake quoting Scriptures as the Holy Ghost prayed for me through unknown tongues. Being connected to the Spirit really propelled me toward a much-needed supernatural healing from God. I had ups and downs, especially the first year, as the kingdom of darkness truly attempted to steal my life. I relied heavily on my parents, the written Word, and my church. God and strong family support were my anchors as I fought to move forward mentally. I did have physical signs of losing weight, loss of appetite, and decreased energy levels, but in all honesty, the mental side offered the greatest battles of my life. I think people process events differently, but for me, coping with divorce in my early twenties hit me like a ton of bricks.

As the old western saying goes, my family "circled the wagons" around me to help me through this difficult time. Each one of them were there for me in their own unique ways. For example, my brother-in-law Mark and I went shooting at a local gun range, a hobby that both of us enjoy. I can remember him picking me up in his Jeep, loading up our stuff, rolling the windows down, cranking the worship music up, and just cruising down the highway as the wind hit our faces. In those moments, it made me forget about everything and just feel alive. The smell of pine trees in the woods, the sound of a cartridge being loaded into the chamber, and the comradery of being with guys on the range made for a great day.

As I look back now, I know that my family did a lot of those things to help me cope with the whirlwind in my life. Family support during life-changing circumstances is priceless in this world. I leaned on them heavily for biblical advice, prayer, and loving support because I truly trusted them. Some days, I needed a hug from my parents or a text from my sister Shannon, and credit to them, they were there in those moments. All the encouraging words helped me mend, and it is true, death and life are in the power of the tongue. I thank God for a strong spiritual family that spoke life over me! Their words uplifted my inner man, and their unwavering love will never be forgotten.

> "A word fitly spoken is like apples of gold in pictures of silver." – Proverbs 25:11

A Young Confession

Being wise and making sound decisions as a teenager or young adult can spare one from much trouble. Staying away from pornography, ungodly partners, and youthful lusts can provide a strong foundation for doing things the right way. If I would have been spiritually smart as a teenager, I would have saved myself much heartache. To allow you as the reader to fully grasp our story, I have to confess my ignorance. As a late teenager, I thought a lot about relationships. My parents were married at the age of eighteen, and my sister married her husband Mark at the age of twenty. So, one evening after meeting for a fast-food date, I walked out into the parking lot and heard God say, "Wait, I have someone for you." Being young and really learning to follow God's voice on my own, I paced back and forth. The winter wind pierced my coat, and I remember the parking lot lights glowing down on the black asphalt, as I looked down at my shoes. After some time, I dismissed the words, convinced myself that it must be my own thinking, and left the restaurant.

Over the years, I have looked back at that moment in time and know that my flesh tricked my spirit man. God had a divine plan for me that required me to wait on

Him, but I began to pursue things my own way. Even though I had a heart after God, had a strong commitment to church, attended Christian youth conferences, gave tithes and offerings, and strived to remain out of sin, I made a costly spiritual mistake. Learning to truly follow God's voice for oneself is something that requires much time. It is my belief that the largest percentage of Christians do not know God's voice. One can be saved, on their way to Heaven, and still not know God's voice.

Now I did not blatantly say "No, God," but when the still small voice resounded in me, I struggled to determine if God really said it. The decision to dismiss the words put me on a different road than God had in mind. Being in God's permissive will is much different than being in His divine will. In the New Testament, this is where grace applies itself. When one is trying to live for God wholeheartedly, especially young people, grace covers them until they grow into spiritual maturity. If I would have been smart at that crossroad as a teenager, though, I believe Amanda and I would have met earlier in life. At the age of thirty-two now, I see things much differently than I did then as a teenager.

Is sharing this publicly uncomfortable? Indeed. You have no idea! Who would want to share for the world to read that they had missed God's voice? Knowing the past cannot be changed, I share my story with transparency for not only the backdrop of our testimony, but to help Christians around the world. When in doubt or uncertainty, stand still. Do not press forward unless you know God's will. It is a terrible thing to miss God or take things into your own hands. Sarah's handmaiden birthed out Abraham's son Ishmael, and we currently see Israel still fighting against that mistake. There are always consequences to walking ahead and trying to self-fulfill God's will.

Be patient and check your spirit to validate whether or not it's truly God. Make sure it's not your flesh speaking, make sure it's not a demon, and be positive that it is God communicating with you. Once you're positive, move forward. In my experiences over the years, God often confirms what one knows in their spirit by another godly person. I share my mistake as a teenager openly so young adults can learn from my experience.

In my early thirties now, I know God's voice very well. I can be at work, loading groceries into the trunk, mowing the lawn, preaching behind the pulpit, or anything of the like, and I know when He speaks. It can be in still moments or when life is very busy, and I hear His words. I have to say, though, this has taken many years to develop. With guidance from my dad, I have learned to communicate with God on a regular basis. Being filled with the Holy Ghost, with the evidence of speaking in unknown tongues, I see into the supernatural as well. I have visions where God opens up my spiritual eyes to warn me of upcoming events or things pertaining to my family, for example.

Do I say this to pump myself up and display how spiritual I am? Absolutely not. I share my walk with

God to help prove that we can communicate with Him. Being a country boy raised on a farm, if I can learn God's voice, you can as well. If my parents and I would have not been connected to the spiritual realm, Amanda and I would have never known each other existed. Following God in this life requires knowing His still small voice. In Scripture, we find that Elijah knew God on a different level than most people! He knew God's still small voice, and as I testify throughout this book, we can know it as well.

> "And after the earthquake a fire; but the Lord was not in the fire: and after the fire a still small voice." – I Kings 19:12

Hope in Great Distress

In churches across this world, many people use words like "prophetic" as buzzwords to help sell things, convince others they are spiritual, or to truly mislead people. It's similar to how the word "tactical" is used in anything related to firearms, outdoor equipment, clothing, home defense, hats, etcetera; for the word itself helps sell the merchandise. I often laugh when a store has something like a "tactical fork" on their shelf! I see "prophetic" used in much the same way. It is stamped on just about everything these days, and it is hard to read between the lines on what is true and what is untrue.

But with my walk with God, my parents were like two trail guides leading me to my promised land. They are "prophetic," and God did "speak" to them just like He did to me. Together, they received just as much about Amanda as I did while we waited. When they speak prophetically, our whole family and churches across the states listen. Why is that? They have a twenty-year record of being right on target. I could write for a long time on things they have prophesied, and we have all seen them come true. Their prophecies are detailed and well documented. I am extremely grateful to have their godly presence in my life. My mom, who moves in gifts of the Holy Ghost, actually knew things would be happening and changing soon in my life.

About a year before the divorce and return to my parents, God told my mom that I would be moving back into the house. At the time, she did not know exactly what that meant. She did not tell me but had told my dad. They prayed on it for quite some time, and kept the word from the Lord in confidence. But in hindsight, we know God already knew where I would be living for the next few years. He gave them a heads-up and allowed them to mentally prepare themselves for their grown son moving back into the nest. For any parent, that takes a while to sink in, I would think. But even in difficult times, God is not surprised by anything that happens in this world. He sees the future and plans His children for it. He gave my parents a heads-up, and they knew something would be happening. Again, they never said a word to me until after the divorce.

My mom, with regards to our family especially, moves in the gift of prophecy. She loves the family being unified, and God graciously allows her insight into things that pertain to my sister and me. She is not very outspoken with what she knows, but when the time comes, she declares boldly what God has given her. I am very grateful to God for giving them a warning of the whirlwind that continued to gain speed.

When the time came, I began moving all my belongings to my parents' upstairs loft in their country A-frame home. I unpacked suitcases, emptied bags of clothes, arranged the room, and tried to mentally grasp the whirlwind that had just happened. I often caught myself staring at random things, and sitting alone with a great sense of numbness. I felt as if I were hit by a large truck but had no physical trauma. I set my toothbrush up in my parents' bathroom, put my dirty clothes at the foot of their washer, and used their house like my own. Moving back into the nest offered weird feelings for me, to say the least. I never thought I would move back into my parents' home, especially under those circumstances. I remember going to a store to buy a movable closet rack to hang my clothes. All my clothes were at the foot of my bed, and my belongings were stashed along the wall. It paints quite the picture. I gave all my large furniture away since I did not have any room in my new bedroom. I used boxes and plastic totes to store my belongings. My set-up resembled a studio apartment. I prayed to God out of the window in the photo below many nights.

I am truly giving you the play-by-play as it happened. I cannot add or take away from the story. It glorifies God more to lay it all out and show transparency in every aspect. In the first few days at living with my parents, I remember sitting out by their firepit area. We built this place for our summer cookouts, and to build bonfires on cool fall nights. I had my feet propped up on some large rocks as I sat in an old lawn chair. At this fire pit, God changed my life.

In that moment, I told God that if it be His will, I would never be married again nor seek a relationship. I would preach the gospel my whole life, live alone, be sexually abstinent, and never change my view on the matter. In simple words, I explained to Him that I would be single for the rest of my days. I cannot convey to you how genuine this prayer came from my heart, and only God heard that prayer. I did not speak it out loud but prayed in the deepest caverns of my spirit man. Thank goodness God knows the thoughts and intents of the heart.

As I sat there quietly after letting God know where my heart's loyalty stood, God specifically told me in my spirit, "Stay here and don't move, and I will bring you a wife." The news hit me straight on, and it came unexpectedly. I sat there motionless as I attempted to wrap my head around His words. I received a command and a promise simultaneously from the Lord Almighty very early in the healing process. While I was still numb from the divorce, God blindsided me in a good way with hope in such a time of distress. God often gives a promise with a command. It's like He says something will happen if you obey and do what He says to do. Remember, direct obedience is easy! I knew God had my life in His hands, and hearing His words boosted my inner man. No matter what one is going through, when God speaks, it is a game changer. On this particular day, I still remember the details like it happened yesterday.

Immediately after my alone time with God, I stepped into the front door of my parents' living room. We were going somewhere that evening to change the scenery of being at home, and I needed to shower quickly to be ready on time. I began taking my shoes off by the front door, and with no mention of what God had just told me, my dad spoke to me as he leaned back in his recliner. God told me to tell you, "I will bring you another woman." I received my confirmation answer quickly from a very anointed man, and I believe God told me early in the four years at my parents' so I would have hope. I shared my word from the Lord with them, and we embraced the positive news.

From this moment on, this hope kept me marching forward and focused on God's will. I had rough days, and I went through many things emotionally and spiritually, but having hope for a better life always resounded in my spirit like a steady drumbeat. It kept me going, and I would repeat God's words constantly. Anytime someone would dare speak negative about my life, I would declare the words from God privately in my spirit.

With this renewed sense of hope, I felt impressed to make a vow to God that I would keep until Amanda and I met. It lined up perfectly with God's will for my life. If He desired me to be single, so be it. But He had other plans, and I embraced them. I told God specifically, whether it would be one year or ten years down the road, I would not date. Scripture tells us that we must not vow anything unto the Lord unless we plan to keep it.

> "When thou vowest a vow unto God, defer not to pay it; for he hath no pleasure in fools: pay that which thou hast vowed." – Ecclesiastes 5:4

My heart became fixed, and I would not back down from my promise. I knew without a doubt that God would keep His Word. Now it became entirely up to me to keep mine. I knew the significance of this vow, and set in my heart to always remain committed. Many people tried to set me up on dates, and I had folks tell me to visit dating websites, but the vow laid deep in my heart to remain single. I stayed focused, teaching every

Sunday, and continued to grow in my spiritual walk with God. I hung out with my parents mostly on the weekends, and seldom went anywhere that involved other people who were not related to me. I invested my time with God, and enjoyed being a hermit to the social world.

Before our church congregation, I submitted my vow as well. I actually announced my vow from our pulpit one Sunday morning, and everyone in attendance knew I refused to date. I only desired to date the woman God had for me and no one else. To be honest with you, many thought I took things too far. Even people who knew me well. But I knew what God had said, and with my confidence in Him, I would tell anyone what He had planned for me. It became my light at the end of the tunnel, and I strived to obtain His promise.

It's easy to read about Peter walking on water, but when I had to walk on water, so to speak, it took a true walk of faith. We read about all the folks in Hebrews chapter eleven because they had lionlike faith. They pressed forward and would not be denied, nor let their faith waver. I had the same mindset, and built a fortress around my thoughts. If God could bring Boaz and Ruth together, He could bring Amanda and me in His timing. His perfect timing took almost four years for us! I told our congregation, because when it eventually happened, I desired them to specifically remember I foretold it years prior. This gives God more credit!

While waiting on God to provide more details, I quickly found out that some people are not excited when God is going to do something great in one's life. Joseph's brothers were not thrilled about Joseph receiving the coat of many colors nor when they heard of his dreams from God. People often lay in wait for one to fail and laugh secretly if it happens. Do not expect everyone to pray for you, do not expect people to cheer you on, and do not expect people to fight your battle. Some of the greatest battles you will ever face in life, you will fight alone. Joseph eventually had his dreams come to pass just as God foretold. But not until after his brothers faked his death, threw him to the bottom of a pit, and sold him to a traveling caravan. And after all of those events, he even had a woman lie about him trying to become sexual with her. What does this tell us? Just because one has a promise directly from the throne room does not mean they will not go through anything. But if they stay close to God, they will prevail to see the promise become reality. If one truly hears from God, they will be fiercely dedicated to seeing it happen. This is normally a factor in determining if one has truly heard from God or if they are just chasing the desires of their flesh. Emotions and feelings will send one on wild goose chases!

Living with my parents did have many advantages that I did not realize then as much as I do today. The loving support and wise counsel brought security into my life. My dad prayed me through many nights, and my mom made the transition the best it could be considering the circumstance. I never really felt alone, and could always count on two godly people who lived it at home just like they did at church. And I have to admit, my mom did my laundry and fixed me those amazing homecooked meals. Coming in the front door after work, smelling chicken and dumplings with chocolate chip cookies for dessert, would boost the morale of just about anyone. It felt nice having comforts and being able to enjoy some of my childhood favorites. We would go on drives in the evenings, go fishing at some local ponds, and go on walks up and down our country road. Now looking back, it's amazing how God tucked me away at my parents so I could properly heal and regain my self-worth.

Leaving Dark Days Behind

May an individual marry after a divorce, scripturally? It quickly became the million-dollar question in my life that I had to answer with the Bible. Lining up with Scripture is always the focal point that Christians must press toward, and as a young man, questions arose in my spiritual walk with God. I knew what God had told my pastors and me about sending another woman, but I began to research in great depth the written Word. Understand with great clarity, God's Ramah words will never contradict His written Word. I strived to be accurate in my understanding of remarriage.

As I lived in my parents' home under a command from God, I continually read the writings of Apostle Paul in the first book of Corinthians. In addition, I studied Old and New Testament Scripture with the wise counsel of my dad to cross-reference verses. One must understand that biblical grounds for divorce are clear, and do not apply to the largest percentage of couples who part ways. The verses below line up with others, and even though I can go into further detail, it's not the purpose of this book. But I do want to highlight a few verses that are at the forefront of the topic. In regards to moving forward in my life, it brought a great sense of peace to know that Scripture lined up with God's spoken words to us.

A person can be loosed from a marriage covenant if the grounds for divorce line up with the written Word of God. A covenant is always conditional as Scripture reveals. Marriage, much like our salvation covenant, is till we take our last breath unless one breaks the covenant. If one rebels on God, the salvation covenant is broken. In the same respect, if one breaks the marriage covenant through sin and leaves, the "till death do us part" is annulled. I am a firm believer in the doctrine of backsliding and it's a great parallel to a biblical divorce. In addition, if remarriage sent people to Hell, God wouldn't have orchestrated His divine plan for Amanda and me in the first place. He would have never spoken to my pastors and me about Amanda for four years either. He would have accepted my pledge of singlehood by the fire pit, and that would have been the end of the story. I am living proof that one can leave dark days behind through the mercies of God and remarry.

Having studied the topic for many years, I love how clear Scripture is. I share some verses below, and expound on them as well.

> "But if the unbelieving depart, let him depart. A brother or sister is not under bondage in such cases: but God hath called us to peace." – I Corinthians 7:15

If the unbeliever decides to leave the marriage covenant, walks out on their spouse, and forsakes Christianity, the Bible says to let them go. In this specific case, the spouse left is no longer under bondage or bound by the marriage covenant. Due to being released, they can remarry without being in sin. This verse protects the one left, and does not punish them their entire lives for the wrongdoing of another. Now, peace can truly follow the separation.

> "Art thou bound unto a wife? seek not to be loosed. Art thou loosed from a wife? seek not a wife. But and if thou marry, thou hast not sinned; and if a virgin marry, she hath not sinned. Nevertheless, such shall have trouble in the flesh: but I spare you." – I Corinthians 7:27-28

If you are currently in a marriage, do not seek to be loosed. If you have been loosed from the covenant, do not seek a wife. As Apostle Paul mentioned in other verses, it became his hope that all remain single just like him. Not only for spiritual purposes, but also in that day, persecution against Christians intensified. Followers were losing their lives, and it served one better to not have a family to protect while ministering. Then it says, "But even if you do marry, you have not sinned." This means if you meet a Christian, and it be God's will, if you do remarry after being divorced (loosed), you have not sinned.

"But I say unto you, That whosoever shall put away his wife, saving for the cause of fornication, causeth her to commit adultery: and whosoever shall marry her that is divorced committeth adultery." – Matthew 5:32

Fornication in the Bible is clearly a reason for separation. Many study Bibles break down the word "fornication" and it is not always sexual. But unfaithfulness or stepping outside the covenant for extra-marital affairs is a reason for divorce. If one breaks the covenant by doing so then one is not under bondage any longer. Although a marriage can be restored after an affair, the victim is not required to remain with that person—especially when the person leaves and marries another.

In the first two verses listed above, it clearly reads that a person can become divorced on biblical grounds and then ultimately marry again. In this instance, they have not sinned, have permission to marry a Christian, and can continue on with God. Having been through a divorce as a young man, I seek to encourage and help believers who have been through similar circumstances. Some want to tar and feather Christians who have been divorced, say their life is over. Yet sometimes there are individuals who are trying to do things God's way.

As mentioned above, Apostle Paul says in I Corinthians 7:15, "But if the unbelieving departs, let him depart. A brother or a sister is not under bondage in such cases: but God hath called us to peace." So, this particular verse covers a brother or sister who has been left by their spouse. They can still be in right standing with God if the other spouse freely chooses not to follow God, forsakes Christianity, and leaves the marriage covenant. If an individual is truly supposed to live in "peace," as it says, then they must let them depart. Think about it, a person cannot physically restrain someone from leaving a marriage covenant, and even if they did, this is not peace. A victim should not be punished their whole lives for the wrongdoings of another, especially when the one who left remarries. And of course, a person cannot commit suicide if one leaves them or they will wake up in Hell.

As Christians, we must look closely at what the Word states in regards to the tragedy of a divorce. It is the moral compass of the world, and if we follow it closely, God provides great detail on marriage and divorce. His commandments and laws are a binding contract, and I am a firm believer in following them with all diligence. In many cases, a divorce cannot be granted due to it not meeting the standards outlined throughout Scripture. In these instances, the couple needs to work their differences out, pray to have their marriage restored, possibly separate for a season, and fully attempt to work toward reconciliation.

As a church, knowing how to operate and govern scripturally in regards to the lives of people is paramount in being well pleasing to God. With so many people broken and hopeless, we must attempt to reach the ones who are considered by some to be the "black" sheep of the flock. When in fact, this small percentage of believers followed Scripture precisely. I suppose if past hardships disqualify someone from being a Christian in right standing with God, we would have no five-fold ministry, no testimonies, and zero churches. Some of the greatest people of God who have walked this world have incredible stories of how God pulled them from gutters and raised them up to bring Him glory.

How about the ones who have sinned in their life, but seek to be put back into right standing with God? As Christians, we are commanded to love and forgive in this present world. If we bash people up against the head all the time for sins in their past or tragedies in their lives, none of us would be good enough to be followers of Christ. There are always consequences to sin, losses in tragedies, but even if you are the one who committed the sin, there is hope. Millions of divorces have happened since the beginning of time, and even if you were in the wrong, the redemptive power of Jesus can set you free. Maybe you committed adultery, maybe you slept around before marriage, maybe you watched pornography; what do you do in these cases? Truly repent, which means turn away from your sin, dust yourself off, commit yourself to a "Book of Acts" type of church every time the doors are open, put God first in everything you do, and follow Him who will cast your sins into the depths of the sea.

> "He will turn again, he will have compassion upon us; he will subdue our iniquities; and thou wilt cast all their sins into the depths of the sea." – Micah 7:19

At our home church, we preach extremely hard against all sin. Several have left our church over the years due to prophecy, strong sermons, and infallible truth. One will either become a stronger disciple in our church or they will ultimately quit. There is not much gray area because sin is a life and death situation. At the same time, on the flip side of saving with fear, we show incredible grace and love toward the ones who have messed up. It is our desire to lead people into right standing with God whether they are first-time converts or backslidden individuals.

> "And of some have compassion, making a difference: And others save with fear, pulling them out of the fire; hating even the garment spotted by the flesh. Now unto him that is able to keep you from falling, and to present you faultless before the presence of his glory with exceeding joy." – Jude 22-24

Let me share this story with you. On an ordinary day, God spoke to my dad to quickly rush to a house where a recently divorced man lived. Upon arrival, my dad frantically beat on the door of the house. As the door slowly opened, my dad saw a handgun sitting on the table. The man wanted to commit suicide because he could not handle the depression, the thoughts, and the struggles of what had just happened. Out of love, God sent my dad to stop the tragedy. The man received another chance to serve God. Knowing God's voice is paramount in this present world! No matter the circumstance, God still has redemptive plans of a bright future for those who decide to turn to Him.

Name Given

God's plan emerged rather quickly once I moved back in with my parents. I remember sitting in the front seat of their Honda Civic one afternoon. We had loaded up to take off, and I remember grabbing the gear shift to put the car in drive. When from the back seat, my mom asked me if the name "Amanda" meant anything to me. I can remember looking at her through the rearview mirror and responding, "No, not particularly." She said, "Well, God wants you to start praying about it." Little did I know, this name would change my life.

At the time, we did not know what it meant exactly, but it did spark conversations in the car. I kept thinking of Amanda's whom I went to school with, women named Amanda in churches, and we rattled off a few between one another. I did not know my future wife's name would be Amanda at the time, but I knew it had significance or God wouldn't have mentioned it. God always has a purpose for things. He is not the author of confusion nor does He randomly speak with no substance to His words. So, I took the words seriously, and prayed on the name. I did think it had quite the ring to it and went well with my last name!

One night, about a week later, I laid by myself next to the wood burner in my parents' living room. Being around ten o' clock, my parents had already gone to bed. All sprawled out on the living room floor, I prayed and meditated on God's Word. The stillness of the house, the sound of coyotes howling in the woods outside, helped my heart be very still as I listened for God. As I lay there for quite some time, I felt my heart become warm as God's presence entered the room. I best describe it as a hot ember sitting on top of my heart. As I felt His presence emerge into the room, I heard God say in a still small voice, "Amanda Gill." And simultaneously, I saw it written out in an open vision with a cursive style text. My mom had received Amanda first, and now it became confirmed to me with the last name as well. I told my parents the very next morning, and we now had a name.

God used two people to receive one name. Knowing the name of the woman brought great excitement into my life to say the least, and we called her "A" or "AG" for short. I can remember sitting by the firepit many nights, and my family would jokingly say, "Wonder what "AG" is doing right now?" I looked at the stars during the night from my loft window, and knew Amanda slept somewhere underneath those same stars. I began praying for her, pleading the blood of Jesus over her, and asked God to continually draw her close to Him. In a way, I felt connected to Amanda due to my prayers before we ever met.

I mean, here I am praying for a woman whom I had never even seen before. How wild is that? Let me tell you, it takes great faith to believe in something of this magnitude. Here I am, following God down a path for an unknown woman named Amanda Gill. Talk about a thrill ride! One just cannot make this stuff up, folks. And God, who loves to confirm things, spoke to three different people about what He had planned in the future. The whole family knew we were waiting on Amanda Gill.

To bring further anticipation into the wait, God told my mom one day that Amanda would be "very beautiful." God started giving us details and descriptions to look for as we progressed early in the process. Some people share testimonies about making it to church on time. Here I am, waiting on a woman whom I have never met before! It is a completely different level, folks. Christians can do mighty things, but they have to raise their faith to achieve mighty things.

I once heard an old saying that goes like this: "Two types of Christians exist: one group pecks with the chickens and the other soars with the eagles." Basically, God will perform in your life by how much you line up with His Word, and what you are able to believe for each and every day. One of the worst things a Christian can do is accept their circumstances. God has called us to be victorious, to speak unto the immovable mountains, and to be blessed here on earth. If He can lead Israel by a cloud, make manna appear on the ground for them in the mornings, and make water come spewing out of a rock to quench their thirst, then He can lead and bless us according to our measure of faith.

Bind Up My Wounds, Lord

In the first few months after the divorce, I spent much time out by the wood stacks that we cut for my parents' wood burner. The wood, mostly oak and hickory, that we cut every year supplied a blazing heat even on the coldest nights of the winter. The fresh aroma of a crackling fire on a cold night brought the lovely outdoors right into the house. There between those freshly cut wood stacks, I sat on an old chair as I stared through the woods as the sun glistened on top of the leaves. From here, I watched squirrels play as they chased each other up and down the branches. I heard bob white quail whistle in the distance, and occasionally saw wood ducks land in the marsh down below. Watching the woods come alive as I sat still became therapeutic to me, and I sat there for hours in prayer. I often walked down by the marsh to lay in the fall leaves, just to stare upward at the sky.

The closeness to God that I felt in the woods became a special place for me. I could cry, talk with God, yell, sit motionless, and let God bind up the wounds of my heart. One of my favorite Scriptures during this time that I quoted often is found in Psalms. God mended me together like a puzzle. Piece by piece, He did an inner work on me that put me back together and restored what had been lost. Read this powerful inner healing Scripture below that perfectly illustrates how God heals supernaturally. He gathered the outcasts of Israel and made them whole again!

> "The Lord doth build up Jerusalem: he gathereth together the outcasts of Israel. He healeth the broken in heart, and bindeth up their wounds." – Psalms 147:2-3

Being on a small farm, my dad had horses, chickens, and dogs to keep things interesting. Besides praying in the woods, I began to raise white rock bantam chickens. I built pens for them, and hatched out chicks throughout the summer months. It reminded me of my childhood, and it gave me something to do besides work. I sold the young birds, and kept incubating eggs to renew the flock. I can remember sitting in the old chicken coop as I watched chickens interact with each other.

The simplicity of how they lived became relaxing to me. At such a vulnerable state, I found nature and animals beneficial in coping with my life. I felt God while sitting in an old chicken pen or in the woods leaned up against a stump. I truly believe God used the simple things in life to rehabilitate my emotional well-being. David tended the sheep, Abraham had herds, Peter went fishing, and pesky ravens fed Elijah. God using animals to teach people things is embedded throughout Scripture.

As I look back, I thank God for taking me back to my country roots to mend my heart and prepare me for the road ahead. Without question, if God desired me to be a husband in my lifetime, I had to heal properly. So many are quick to jump from one relationship to the next, but I refused to be worldly. I understood that I had to concentrate on myself in order to be the man God needed me to be. I focused on my inner man, and asked God to heal my heart. Much like a renowned surgeon, He stitched me up and stopped the bleeding. I remember God telling me one day in prayer, "From this day forward, you are healed." Not only did I hear the words, but I felt much different on the inside. It changed my mindset, depression began to leave, and even though I still had to overcome things, I knew God had performed spiritual surgery. I confessed my healing daily and changed my focus. I strived to move forward and leave the past behind. I believed in my inner healing, and did not mope around defeated.

Pastor Don again gave me another prophecy from God following my healing: "Son, I have not called you to fail, but have called you to rise up, and have called you by name." I knew I had to keep fighting and continually go forward. In Ephesians 6, we read about all the military gear of that day in reference to fighting against the devil. Notice there is no protection or armor to protect the back? This is because, as Christians, we are always commanded to go forward, and never called to retreat. We fight moving forward, and in doing so, leave the past behind. Even Apostle Paul knew this truth well, and had to leave his memories of persecuting Christians in the streets of Jerusalem behind. Many Christians always live in the past within their minds, and as they freeze in time, they never do anything great for God. People often hold onto things that happened twenty years ago. Do not do that! Be like Paul, who left his past, and wrote much of the New Testament!

> "Brethren, I count not myself to have apprehended: but this one thing I do, forgetting those things which are behind, and reaching forth unto those things which are before, I press toward the mark for the prize of the high calling of God in Christ Jesus." – Philippians 3:13-14

In my early twenties, I did not have much confidence in living at home. I would run into old high school friends and they would ask, "Where you living these days?" And having to be brutally honest, I replied, "Living at my parents' right now." This wasn't exactly the most glorious thing a man in his early twenties could say. We think that we are going to conquer the world, and when I realized I basically lived in my parents' attic, it took away my confidence. I often received the usual smirk as they told me what they were up to and where they were living. Of course, I remained happy for them. But oh, how I longed to have my own place and family. I usually redirected the conversation, and verbally pushed the story line away from me.

Living with my parents became a humbling experience to say the least. Of course, I am forever grateful for their generosity and am truly indebted to them. But here me out, it's not exactly the coolest thing in the world to be living with parents as an adult. My mom's cooking sure did fatten me up, though. My dad's wise counsel kept me focused, and God knew what He was doing the whole time. Living with folks who are spiritually connected to God has benefits that only true believers understand. It kept me on the straight and narrow path, which eventually led me to Amanda.

In the first few days at my parents', God specifically told me, "Stay here and don't move, and I will bring you a wife." Those words planted deep in my heart, and I knew that I had to stay despite any thoughts of finding my own place. When God gives a command, He is not requesting one to obey. He is telling! I firmly believe, as I look back over those days, my obedience to God positioned me to receive His blessing.

> "And Samuel said, Hath the Lord as great in burnt offerings and sacrifices, as in obeying the voice of the Lord? Behold, to obey is better than sacrifice, and to hearken than the fat of rams." – I Samuel 15:22

The first year at my parents', I experienced a rocky road. Of course, God spoke and I had incredible things to hold onto each and every day. But the struggles were real even with the promise from God. I continually fought ungodly thoughts, dreams, and demonic attacks on my mind. My dad became my anchor during those dark days, and my relationship with him served me well. We listened to music as we lay on the living room floor at night. We opened the living room patio door to let a nice breeze come in as we sang old gospel songs, such as "The Old Gospel Ship," "Moses, Take Your Shoes Off," "Ain't No Grave Gonna Hold This Body Down," and "Looking for a City." We basked in the presence of God as we talked about spiritual things. I asked my dad often when he thought Amanda would come on the scene. We really never knew, and I must have asked him a thousand times as we waited.

I have such fond memories of both of us laying on the floor, with our feet propped up on the couches, listening to the classics. My mom would jokingly yell from her bedroom to turn the music down as we became happy in the Lord. As we pushed into late fall, the fire in that old wood burner crackled and popped. The fresh aroma of hickory and oak just made those nights. Laying by the fire, we sought the Lord, and I will never forget His glorious presence in the middle of that living room.

Quick Notes on Prophecy

To begin, what is prophecy? In simple words, prophecy is a foretold future event given by God to a Christian. It can involve people, places, things, or anything that God wants a person to know. If you have never been exposed to "prophecy" or your church never teaches or operates in it, the concept can be a deep thing to grasp initially. But think about it, it's embedded throughout Scripture, and God at some point in history didn't just stop communicating with us. Notable men and women in the Bible who gave prophecies includes, among others: Miriam, Agabus, Ezra, Nathan, Deborah, Jeremiah, John the Baptist, Elijah, Micah, and Elisha. And it is still true today! We still have true prophets and prophetesses who hear from God. They are the mouthpieces that God supernaturally uses to point the way or warn of upcoming events. They are called to move in this special office to help people know of things in the future.

Whether for a church, a group of people, a family, or an individual, prophecy allows believers to catch a brief glimpse into the mind of God. On a side note, true prophets will always preach or teach the Word on a regular basis. It is one way of many to correctly identify if they are from God. If someone prophesies, but is not deeply embedded in a good church, stay clear!

Secondly, what is the GIFT of prophecy? This free gift is available to anyone baptized in the Holy Ghost with the evidence of speaking in unknown tongues. These folks (just like my mom) can move in the free gift of prophecy, but are not called in the five-fold ministry of being a prophet. The entire list of the nine gifts of the Holy Ghost, including the gift of prophecy, are listed in I Corinthians chapter twelve. Even Apostle Paul says in I Corinthians chapter 13:2, "And though I have the gift of prophecy," which means he operated in this free supernatural gift as well. This gift allows faithful church members who are baptized in the Holy Ghost to prophesy as God leads them. As they share what God gives them, these folks should not interrupt church services, should not seek personal satisfaction, and should wait for God's perfect timing to release what they know to the pastor first, then secondly to someone else. They are called to be very orderly, and do things in submission to the authority of a pastor. But if you have someone in your church who moves in this gift, count yourself blessed! They are true treasures.

My parents have moved in prophecy for over twenty years, and it seems to be increasing as they continue to walk with God toward their destinies. God uses them as mouthpieces to fulfill His will. Much like Moses leading the Israelites in the wilderness on their voyage, God led me by my parents. My dad, who has moved in all nine gifts in his life, operates consistently with God to lead our church, family, and others in the ministry. I have heard him say before that his earthly life is almost boring at times compared to the supernatural side of God. And it makes complete sense to me as I continue to grow in God myself. For spiritual people, this world can become boring. While God saved me from a deep pit, I experienced Him on new levels as well. This life sure is exciting when God is in the mix!

The spiritual world has been here much longer than the physical world. Even Apostle Paul became caught up into the third Heaven after Jesus ascended on high. To experience things outside of the physical realm makes life exciting and captivating. It is like living a double life, but in the most sinless way possible to bring glory to God.

> "If ye then be risen with Christ, seek those things which are above, where Christ sitteth on the right hand of God. Set your affection on things above, not on things on the earth. For ye are dead, and your life is hid with Christ in God." – Colossians 3:1-3

To walk in the spirit while living on earth, a believer must be able to coexist in both worlds. We have to learn to communicate with God who made Heaven and earth, but not neglect our earthly responsibilities. We must go into our prayer closet to fight spiritual battles, and then come down from the spiritual high to do the laundry. This coexisting takes practice! Sometimes, I will be on cloud nine with God after prayer time, and Amanda will say, "Hey, babe, Silas pooped. Can you change him?" So, I move into the physical world to fulfill my fatherly responsibilities! Doing dishes, feeding the chickens, going to work, mowing the lawn, raking leaves, etcetera, but at the same time, serving God with my heavenly responsibilities. So, in my personal life, when I knew that I would marry Amanda one day, I still had to be faithful in the small things as well. I learned how to coexist between the prophetic news and my everyday routine.

Not everyone who prophesies is hearing from God. In fact, in our experiences, false prophecy outnumbers true prophecy by at least a ten to one ratio. False prophecy is like a giant decoy. It is absolutely mindboggling how much of it penetrates the churches of today. Many do not know what to believe because they listen to people who follow demons or their own fleshly ways. Be careful who you listen to, and test whether they are of God or not. Many speak just to hear their own voice, and use "God says" to validate their words. But in reality, God never spoke and people are led astray. Even in the Old Testament, God is very repulsed by people using His name to satisfy their own lusts.

> "Then the Lord said unto me, the prophets prophesy lies in my name: I sent them not, neither have I commanded them, neither spake unto them: they prophesy unto you a false vision and

divination, and a thing of nought, and the deceit of their heart." – Jeremiah 14:14

Two Visions of Amanda

I can see the first vision just as clear today as the first day God gave it to me. It will forever be embedded in my memory. In the vision, I walked into my father's office at church. I saw him sitting behind his desk, and in the two chairs to my left, Amanda and her dad sat there. I knew instantly from God that Amanda stood five feet and six inches tall, had long brown hair, had a slender body type, and appeared very beautiful. As I looked at her dad, I knew he had high energy. He tapped his knee, and I knew that he had a go-getter personality.

These details gave me a visual description of the woman God had for me. I shared these details with my parents. Does God move this precisely? Yes, He does! I am living proof that God is concerned with every aspect of our lives. If He became concerned with the pots and pans of the Israelites in the Old Testament, He is definitely concerned about our relationships.

With these specific details, I knew what to look for when I saw Amanda, and could compare her to the vision. I even saw her dad! And let me tell you, Mike loves life, and has an enthusiastic energy that never quits. He has a high motor, and everyone who knows him can testify of his exuberance. God gives exact details! Having known him for years now, God hit the nail on the head. Mike brings the high energy, and is fun to be around. The description of Amanda hit spot on as well. It's life-changing to know details about things pertaining to this life. My dad really moves in this anointing as well, and his prophecies are not vague, but precise and detailed. Often, false prophets or people who want to act spiritual give non-detailed prophecies so they have a higher chance of not being wrong. But people connected to God have unearthly precision.

My second vision happened not long after the first. In the vision, I stood in a small field, next to a garden area. As I looked around, I saw Amanda crouched down, and motioning me to come look at something on the ground. I remember her long brown hair, but this vision did not offer quite the details as the first one. I knew Amanda had a big smile, and in the vision, she knew me. As I began to walk toward her, the vision ended. I can still see all the details like it happened last night. Green grass blanketed the ground, an old barn stood behind her, and the weather appeared as a beautiful summer day. These two visions burned deep within my heart. I replayed them like movies throughout the day in my memory. To somewhat illustrate, it is like watching a small video clip. It's like you're there and you can see all the details. Even years later, I can still see everything if I begin to think on it. Is God this detailed? He sure is! Amanda has a smile that truly lights up a room. In the visions, years before we met, one of the most detailed descriptions turned out to be her big smile. As a kid, people often called her "Smiles" as a nickname. Again, God gave a very detailed description.

With a name and two descriptive visions, I began to casually search the internet through search engines and social media platforms for women named Amanda Gill. One day, as I searched, I found a profile photo that looked like the woman I had seen in the visions. I showed my dad, and at the time, we just bookmarked the profile. It was bookmarked on our old laptop for at least a year. I strictly went off the name and the visions. I would randomly go back to that profile over the coming months, and wonder if this would turn out to be the true Amanda Gill. I remember browsing through her public photos, and one in particular looked exactly like the woman in the visions. But I did not know for sure at the time, and of course, we were very cautious while waiting on God. I remember seeing a man with her in some photos, and wondered what role he had in her life. At first, I thought she might be with someone. Later on, I found out that her brother Gabriel turned out to be the one in the photos! I felt a divine connection to that profile, and I know God allowed me to find it. Amanda set most of her profile to private, but it had just enough public things for me to scroll through. I truly believe, if we put God first in everything we do, He truly does order our footsteps. Or in this case, order my fingertips!

Spiritual Pressure: Occults

I spent much time wondering if I should include these events in the creation of our love story. It is not exactly the most romantic thing to bring into the mix. My family has dealt with satanic occults for many years, but especially during my time waiting for Amanda. We decided to include the details into the matter since it shows what my family and I went through during those four years. Again, I have to be transparent and fill in the details for one to truly grasp the victories that God gave us.

Witchcraft is very prevalent in southern Illinois. We are close to Carbondale, Illinois, which has always been nationally recognized as a witchcraft hotspot. We have had many encounters, both spiritual and physical, with many who practice this sin. Witches, warlocks, high priests, covens, and occults have come after us for over a decade. Since the beginning, we have stood strong against satanism and all things associated with the religion. We have shined light onto the darkness, and have preached behind the pulpit, on radio stations, and online platforms for years against its agenda.

To be detailed and transparent, I have to include these events due to the added spiritual pressure it brought into my life. I received an onslaught of demonic attacks from many different fronts. For some, this is a surprise. Dealing with occults and witches? To true pastors or people in the ministry, this is often common territory. The devil uses people who serve him to try and disrupt what God is doing. But in our case, they all failed miserably. Hexes, vexes, seances, potions, summoning demons, pentagrams, sacrifices, rituals, and much more intertwine within the wickedness. As messengers of light, we are called to stomp out such spiritual darkness in this present world. Apostle Paul even had a public display of a giant bonfire to burn witchcraft books!

> "Many of them also which used curious arts brought their books together, and burned them before all men: and they counted the price of them, and found it fifty thousand pieces of silver." – Acts 19:19

I am about to share with you one wild experience! In my last semester of graduate school, while dealing with everything mentioned before this chapter, God gave me an open vision one day. In the vision, I saw a blonde-haired woman standing next to a vehicle with the hood up. It appeared as if the vehicle had broken down, and it was not far from my parents' house. Maybe a three-mile driving distance, and I knew this area in the vision very well. God told me specifically, "They will set a trap for you." I remember telling my parents the vision, and I knew God had warned me of an upcoming event. Does

God move this way? Yes! In the book of Acts, the prophet Agabus warned Paul of an upcoming event for a scriptural reference as well.

> "And when he was come unto us, he took Paul's girdle, and bound his own hands and feet, and said, thus saith the Holy Ghost, so shall the Jews at Jerusalem bind the man that owneth this girdle, and shall deliver him into the hands of the Gentiles." – Acts 21:11

Roughly two days later, the vision that God gave me a few days prior happened. Traveling on my way home from class, at about 8:45 one night, I drove down a backroad to my parents' house. Being late, and very dark, no other vehicles were in the area. My family traveled this road often to my parents' house since it offered a shortcut off the main highways. As I turned left onto a long road surrounded by cornfields, I saw emergency lights begin to flash in the distance. As I drove toward the vehicle, the vision and words from God that I received a few days prior came rushing into my spirit. The vehicle appeared to be broken down, and I saw a man standing behind the driver's side door. He had the door open, which took up most of the road. Under normal conditions, I would have rolled down my window to see if they needed help with anything. But with the vision from God resounding within me, I kept my little green truck moving past them.

The man actually stepped toward my truck while waving his hand to try and motion me to stop. I had to drive partially into a field to have enough room to drive by the vehicle. Traveling around thirty miles per hour, I knew not to stop. In passing, I came back on the road, and in the view of my headlights, I saw the blonde-haired woman standing about fifty feet away. They wanted me to stop, but as I turned the corner, I put the pedal to the medal!

I remember calling my dad first thing, and when he answered, I told him they had tried to trap me. He said that some of them had been yelling from the tree line. My parents actually had satanic occult members yelling at the house. Did they mean to give me harm that night? Yes. Did God protect my family and me? Absolutely. Naysayers will say this does not happen! But oh my, it does. We have lived it for many years, and have so many real-life stories, it would shock the average Christian.

Another evening as my parents and I returned from grocery shopping, we were unloading the car. My dad and I would bring the groceries in and my mom would put them away. As we walked back and forth on the walkway with groceries in hand, my mom yelled from inside the house that rocks were hitting the windows. And sure enough, we could hear rocks hitting the glass. For a few seconds, it was odd because we thought: Who in the world would be doing that? And as we walked on the side of the house by the woods, no one was in sight. As we walked up on the deck, we could see all the rocks laying there from falling down from the windows. My dad and I yelled to see if anyone answered us, but no one responded. In the Holy Ghost, God told my dad they were hiding in the cornfields next to an old fence row. We had many encounters with them before, and knew it was not just someone playing a prank.

In my time living with my parents, we experienced so much hate from members of the kingdom of darkness. Rocks were thrown at the house. We received threatening phone calls, watched warlocks lurk in the woods, and had witches come to church. Vehicles were parked on our road late at night, and people followed us home from church. All these things were happening while I waited for the woman whom I had never met before. Just because I had this grand promise did not mean that I could exempt myself from all the attacks.

God often shows us the end result, but does not show us all the mud we will have to go through to arrive there. It's like He shows us the palace, but not all the miles we must walk before seeing it. The devil often tries to hinder or destroy what God is doing in our lives. His distractions are meant to throw us off course. But hallelujah, we can whip him at his own game! We just worship and praise God despite the circumstances! We always knew in the spirit that these occults were constantly trying to cast evil things on us. We learned really quick how to combat such wickedness.

> "For the weapons of our warfare are not carnal, but mighty through God to the

pulling down of strong holds." – II
Corinthians 10:4

We worshipped, prayed, fasted, took communion,
quoted Scriptures, buried printouts of Psalms 91 in the
four corners of the property, and would not give into
pressure. One time, my sister and mother even saw a
gentleman in a black cape jump into a pickup truck by
the house. He must have been out there all night, and
they came to pick him up. You might say, why haven't
you called the police? Because no crime has been
committed, and it is more of a spiritual battle than a
physical one. Besides, could you imagine trying to
explain this to someone who knows nothing about
spiritual things? God has always warned and protected
us, and we honestly believe it is just a part of being in
the ministry. One night as I sat by my parents' wood
stove, I had a vision of angels being encamped all
around the house. Like a mighty army, they were there
to protect. My family had many angels visit us during
this time. Do guardian angels exist? Yes! Thank the
Lord Almighty for His protection plan.

How about the members of the occults? We pray for
their salvation. I have seen people in occults come to
know Jesus. The power of witchcraft is really a low
level of spiritual living, and once people truly
experience Jesus, they realize how much they are
missing. In Scripture, Simon the sorcerer received the
free gift of salvation.

> "Then Simon himself believed also: and
> when he was baptized, he continued with
> Philip, and wondered, beholding the
> miracles and signs which were done." –
> Acts 8:13

Hallelujah! Simon changed his eternal home in Hell to an eternal paradise in Heaven. He bewitched the people with sorcery for many years, but when Phillip came strolling through with more power, he switched sides. We have the same desire for anyone involved in witchcraft. They need Jesus just like any other sinner. He awaits them with arms open wide. The real supernatural power is with the Heavenly Kingdom!

Gifts of Faith

While waiting, I did not become stagnant. I let my faith arise and put it into action. We know Scripture tells us, "Faith without works is dead, being alone." So, one thing I did every Christmas included buying Amanda a gift. Shopping for a woman whom I had never even met in person! In Christmas 2011, which was the first year at my parents, I bought Amanda a Christmas ornament with her name engraved on it. I remember walking through the Carbondale mall as everyone hustled to find gifts, and seeing a booth that customized ornaments. Not knowing what to buy or what Amanda even liked, I picked an arctic penguin with a small hat. The sales lady asked me what I wanted engraved on the ornament, and as she sat there waiting on my response, I said, "2011 Amanda." This ornament sparked my ever-growing faith! I purposefully had the year put on the ornament because I wanted to look back years later and know that I bought it way before we met.

Sounds cool now, but back then in that mall all by myself, it took a great leap of faith. The next Christmas, I bought Amanda perfumes, body sprays, and lotions. I smelled all the different "try me" bottles and picked out fragrances that I thought she would like. Sales associates would often ask me, "Buying for someone special?" I would respond, "Yes, indeed!" I never told them these gifts were for a woman I had never even met. I thought that would be just a little much for them or they would think I was one weird fantasy dude. I eventually bought Amanda a diamond necklace, a diamond bracelet, a glass rose, and a pink cross bracelet. I kept adding to my collection, and as time went by, the gift sacks kept stacking up. Every so often, I would dust the gifts off, open them to make sure everything remained as before, and change the wrapping paper. Those gifts were in my room on that movable metal closet the whole time. Buying them really propelled my faith into deep waters.

I truly trusted in God, and showed Him my continual faith in what He said. It takes great faith to buy gifts every year by following only prophecy.

My mother also bought Amanda a gift in direct obedience. One day while she walked across the living room floor while doing laundry, God told her to buy Amanda a specific type of perfume. My mom had never even heard of the brand name before so she did a quick search online. As she looked for it, she noticed that a store close by carried the perfume. While my parents were out grocery shopping, they picked it up. Till this day, I remember my mom giving it to me. We kept it with all the other gifts. Not only did I move in faith, but my mom did as well. I love this about our story! We had three people moving in the Spirit toward a promise from God.

These minor details add so much validity to our story. God is not the author of confusion, but instead the author of confirmation. I could not wait to present all these gifts to Amanda. It is surreal to buy something for someone and years later give it to them. The receipts that I kept show the dates that I purchased the items as well. To the best of my ability, I kept a record of the journey so I could one day point the spotlight back to my Lord and Savior.

Finishing My Degree

As the fall season began, my last semester of graduate school hit full stride. Having enrolled in college right after graduating high school, this became my sixth consecutive year of college. I am a proud student of home schooling, mostly through grade school and high school. So yeah, school to me offered a way of life. I held high honors in my classes, and kept a solid grade point average. But in my last semester, I had a hard time focusing on schoolwork with all the mental pressure happening in my life. Dealing with the aftereffects of the divorce, going through spiritual pressure from occults, and living in a loft at my parents put heavy weight on my shoulders. To attend class, do homework, and keep a steady job, while keeping myself afloat mentally and spiritually, took some perseverance. I worked as a graduate assistant for web support services on campus then attended night classes three nights a week. Graduate level homework is intense, and I often pulled all-night study sessions. This last semester offered the greatest obstacles in all my days of schooling. It required so much from me, but with God's grace, I kept trudging forward to finish my master's degree in Education with a concentration in Student Personnel.

While attending a liberal university, my Christian views were commonly attacked. With the way I wrote my papers, how I responded in group discussions, and how I presented my firm beliefs in presentations, I quickly became the focal point of mockery. One night, I had a professor call me up front to answer questions regarding my educational background. He, being an atheist and pro-choice, did not like my biblical stance on the topics at hand. I can remember everyone staring at me so I thought to open the discussion wide open. I explained that my parents home-schooled me in my early years, and my professor almost fell out of his seat. He responded, "You were home-schooled?" with great emphasis, and I said, "Yes" with a smile. He responded, "That explains a lot," and asked me to be seated.

In the same class, a woman wrote a paper on Jesus only being a fairy tale. She did not like me, and wrote the paper out of spite against my faith. Not only the professor, but several in class shared the same sinful viewpoints. Another night in a different class, I had a man get in my face with my stance on abortion. I do not support murder, and know life begins at conception. I based my answers solely on Scripture, and I am the type of person who does not bend on moral issues. It did not go well in that class to say the least, and I thought they would literally stone me if it wasn't for the laws of the land. I learned that the ones who scream for tolerance are not so tolerant themselves.

With all this going on in my life, it became a lot to deal with on a weekly basis. But normally, the Word of

God will either start a revival or a riot, so I took the brunt of the riot. Hopefully, in my calm demeanor and truth speaking of the Word, I planted a spiritual seed into some of them. I pray that they discover their errors one day and come to know Christ. Having been in some type of school for over twenty years, it felt good to finally be done. It did bother me to some degree for it's hard being in classes where people see you as the bigot. But with all the pressure in class and out of class, I continued to grow in my spiritual walk with God. Those liberal classes are there to reeducate young people, and I live to tell about it. Many go to college and come back different. Thanks be to God for strong roots in the Word. I went as a Holy Ghost-filled man and left the same way. That December, I leaped for joy because my college career ended. I remember driving off campus in my little green truck, and never wanted to take another college course again.

Through this time, God never left me. He remained constant, and I felt His peace in the midst of a storm. He carried me as I relied on Him like no other time in my life. I can testify that He truly does stick closer than a brother. I continually talked to Him and never ceased to pray. He became my lifeline on a whole new level, and without Him, I really had no desire to even step foot out of bed in the mornings. A Scripture that I quoted often before stepping out of bed is by King David. This verse has a special place in my heart because my dad quoted it in faith when doctors gave him no hope. Like David, he did not faint, and believed in the land of the living. As I battled whirlwinds myself, I relied heavily on the same Scripture.

> "I had fainted, unless I had believed to see the goodness of the Lord in the land of the living. Wait on the Lord: be of good courage, and he shall strengthen thine heart: wait, I say, on the Lord." – Psalm 27:13-14

I honestly do not know how people continue on without God. This life is but a vapor, appears for a little time, and then vanishes away. Not only do Christians have fire insurance from Hell, but we have God who sticks closer than a brother. I dream about walking the streets of gold one day, standing by the crystal sea, eating of the tree of life, talking with all the patriarchs of old, but I understand that I need God right now. Without Him, I do not know if I would have made it this far in life. He is my safety net, and I am confident because He is by my side. I hope for a better tomorrow because His promises endure forever. Not only in this life, but in the one to come.

While waiting on Amanda, I believed that I would have a beautiful wife, children, and a house of my own, and all this belief came through my faith in what God said. It's not enough to know what He says, but we have to believe what He says as well. Our belief in His Word promotes action. People can say they believe all they want, but if they have no works mixed with their faith, it is similar to an automobile with no gasoline. We must put our faith to action! God sees faith, hears faith, and feels faith, scripturally. Make sure He knows you are walking in faith so He can reward you accordingly!

> "Likewise, also was not Rahab the harlot justified by works, when she had received the messengers, and had sent them out another way? For as the body without the spirit is dead, so faith without works is dead also." – James 2:25-26

A Is Coming

My dad jogged in the mornings down our country road, and he always came in all hot and sweaty. I ate breakfast that morning in the house, and like always, he came busting through the door in his usual style. At this time, I had been living with my parents around three years since my initial move to the upstairs loft. With a smile on his face, He said that while he jogged God had spoken to him, saying "A is coming." Well I began to shout for joy as I stood up, ran around the house like a wild monkey, and leaped for joy. I had such an inner excitement within my heart that I had not felt in a long time. God in all His splendor had announced that Amanda Gill would be coming onto the scene.

I remember trimming my beard, putting extra cologne on, and staying well-dressed after that day. I had no idea when we would meet or where. I thought maybe the grocery store, maybe at a sporting event, maybe she would walk right into our church, or maybe God just gave her my phone number. All these thoughts filled my head! Did she even know anything about me? Had God been giving her things on me as well? All I know is, in the fall of year 2015, God blessed us with the news of Amanda coming into my life. Every time I went somewhere, I looked for her like a young kid searching for a new toy. While looking down aisles and scanning people coming through doors, I anticipated that we would run right into each other.

But, with all the excitement, the devil planted a trap. He waited until the very end to try and derail what God had planned for our lives. The devil walks up and down in the earth, uses his demons to do his will, and strives to break up what God is about to do. I do not lift the old serpent up, but I am mindful of his tactics. People receive promises from God through prophecies, and the devil hears about them as well. He fights to keep the believer from receiving anything good from God. Even Apostle Paul mentions hindrances by the enemy.

> "Wherefore we would have come unto you, even I Paul, once and again; but satan hindered us." – I Thessalonians 2:18

The old serpent works overtime trying to stop progress and block the path to God's divine will. I believe the devil knew Amanda would be coming on the scene as well. He loathed the idea, and came up with a plot in a last-ditch effort to stop it.

The Decoys

A common trap of the devil is to send a decoy before the real promise steps onto the scene. In ministry, we have seen this happen often. For example, before someone lands the job God has for them, the devil will send a decoy job that requires them to work on Sundays. He temporarily blesses them with a much-needed job just to draw them away from God. When if they would just sit tight and walk in faith, God has the correct job lined up for them so they do not miss church services. This happens all the time. Just because something glitters does not mean it is a blessing from God. Remember, the devil temporarily blesses too with his limited control on the earth. If it will send someone to Hell, he does not mind leading them astray by any means necessary. The old serpent is experienced in creating things that mimic God's blessing, but in the end, it consumes like a hungry lion. Always be watchful and wise to not fall for his trickery. And thanks be to God, for Amanda and I both stepped right over the trap designed to delay everything!

A lady who once visited our church called me about three weeks before Amanda and I met. Being sincere, she told me about this wonderful dream she had of me the night before. In the dream, she said I was with a woman that she knew, and God had put us together. We were close in age, and God would begin setting things up. In the dream, I played the drums on our worship team, and this woman sang as we worshipped God. I listened for some time, and as she ended her description of the dream, I asked the name of the woman. She told me, and I answered, "Not her." She asked, "Are you sure?" I told her God gave me a specific name. She kept persisting that God had indeed spoken; she even had the young woman visit our church. But I held onto the name from God.

I remember one day kneeling down between the chicken pens and barn on one knee as my dad fed the animals. He walked to the barn for more feed and I asked him, "What do I do?" He said, "You already know what to do, and you must wait and hang on to the visions." I rose up from the ground and never looked back. I paused for a moment because I never want to miss God again, but as my spirit checked the dream, it came up invalid. The devil had truly tried to trick me in following a decoy right before Amanda stepped onto the scene.

Listen up, always watch for decoys! They can send you on wild goose chases that waste time, energy, and finances. Obedience is easy but disobedience is extremely complicated. To walk in true obedience, one has to remain focused even when it is not convenient or popular. The lady did not like my response, but oh well, God did. The devil has been around for thousands of years, and his tactics are designed to steal, kill, and destroy. In Scripture, though, we learn to defend ourselves from his tricks, schemes, and traps.

Crazy right? The devilish plot thickens. Around the same time, about three weeks prior, Amanda had a gentleman in Sioux City state that he had heard from God. He believed that he would marry Amanda. She sincerely prayed about the proclamation, but it came up invalid as well. Her spirit did not bear witness with his. Almost simultaneously, in two different states, the devil tried to throw God's divine plan off course. I repeat, be careful of decoys! If we would have been ensnared by the devil, our relationship could have been greatly delayed or possibly never met in the first place. Just because one receives a promise does not mean they will see or experience it. It must be walked out until it comes to fruition. Amanda and I were wise and connected to our living God, and we stepped right over the trap from the pit of Hell.

This had been common territory for Amanda for many years. She had many guys try to say "God said" but they only used this phrase to try and date her. Amanda had people try to set her up with guys like a revolving door. But she never felt comfortable with any of them. Amanda even created a profile on a Christian dating website just to see if God would open any doors. She never felt peace with any guy, and did her best to follow God through this time in her life. Amanda wanted to be married to a godly man, have children, and live as a family. I am very thankful that she waited. What a wonderful testimony in a modern culture that does not value godly principles. We live in a society where the covenant of marriage is infringed upon, abstinence is frowned upon, and waiting on "the one" is an anomaly. Amanda has high morals, and I applaud her for holding true to her faith.

For blood-bought Christians, and in our story as an example, I do know that God can have the "one" picked out for single believers. The problem is, the largest percentage of Christians do not sincerely know God's still small voice nor do they know anything about the communication lines between believers and God.

Divine Connection

In the coming weeks, after we sidestepped the traps from the devil, things began to really heat up. Little did I know, and to my surprise, God would go all social media on me and use Facebook. I know, right? I suppose God can use any platform He wants and is not limited to anything. At this time, I did not even have a Facebook page. I always thought too much drama occurred on social media, and I did not have a desire to update my page on a regular basis. I managed our church page, but never desired to have my own.

Not too long after the "A is coming" prophecy, my dad walked into the living room one evening. With ink pen in hand and whiteout on his fingers from handwriting his sermon all day, he strolled to his recliner. He has studied almost every Thursday and Friday since I can remember, and oftentimes comes out of his den to relax in his recliner for a few minutes. Even now, I usually do not disturb my dad on those two days of the week. The whole family knows that he is studying. On this particular day, his routine happened like normal as I sat on the couch checking my email. But things changed suddenly when he began to speak.

I remember sitting on the couch, and he said, "You need to get a Facebook." I can remember responding, "No, I do not want one." He then reiterated, "You need to get a Facebook." He leaned back in his recliner, tapped his fingers, and had this half smile on his face. Knowing my dad very well, I instantly knew that it was a God thing. Once I became certain, I scrambled to open an account. I began creating my profile. I filled out a few things, threw up an old photo of me, and friended a couple people quickly to add some content to my profile.

Once I spent some time establishing this brand-new profile, I asked my dad, "What now?" He responded with a smile on his face, "Friend her." I was totally following my spiritual leader here! Well here we go! The last few years of waiting on Amanda Gill had come to one true moment. I sat there looking at my dad and I was like, "You sure?" I totally made sure he had one hundred percent confidence, but truly in all my years, he has never been wrong, prophetically. Within a moment, I hit the "Send Friend Request" button because God led me in that moment to finally reach out to Amanda. Riding on my dad's confidence, what God had given us, and a pure rush of excitement, we waited for Amanda to respond. I found myself staring at the message screen to Amanda's profile that we had bookmarked on our old laptop for over a year. When a moment of this magnitude happens on an ordinary day, one should know that God is at work.

Within three seconds, Amanda replied, *"Hi there, how do I know you?"* I remember looking at my dad in an amazed look and said, "Now what?" The conversation had begun. Is this really happening? Is this the Amanda that I have been waiting nearly four years for? I remember asking my dad for advice on what to say. We shot some possible phrases back and forth quickly, and finally settled on something generic. My first response verbatim to her is below:

> "Well, we actually do not know each other! Just started a Facebook a while ago, and wanted to add you since you are a Christian. Like the Christian things on your profile. Nice to meet you!"

I refrained from immediately saying that we would be married. Did not want to come off as a creeper, stalker, or some "catfish" from overseas. But boy, my demeanor as I sat on that couch became a mix between a kid in a candy store and my sister opening her birthday gifts. What a rush of excitement! The conversation rolled, and we talked about God, church, our families, and anything to keep the conversation alive. One of the first things I asked Amanda was "How tall are you?" She responded, "I am around 5'6." I knew at that moment she could very well be the woman I would spend the rest of my life with. Nothing to do with me really, but everything to do with being a part of God's plan. All those details that God had given me years ago allowed me to start comparing her to them. I know without a doubt that God detailed things for me so I could use them to clearly identify the true Amanda Gill.

We messaged each other constantly on Messenger those first couple days. We sent photos of our families, churches, vehicles, musical equipment, and anything relevant to our young relationship. We talked about the Bible, and from the very beginning, knew our doctrines had similar understanding of Scripture. This is a divine miracle in itself with so many denominations across the world. Once we started talking, we honestly never stopped. We enjoyed learning about each other and sharing our testimonies with God.

From the very beginning, God told me to be blatantly honest with Amanda. I began to open up about my life like an open canvas for her to view. I told her all about the divorce, how I had been living with my parents for almost four years, and answered any questions that she had for me. And to my surprise, she had never moved out of her parents' home. Instead of living in a loft area, she lived in their remodeled basement. What a relief! God knew the whole time. It eased the embarrassment factor of living under my parents' roof still.

After a few days, we exchanged phone numbers. This way, we could text instead of using Messenger to stay connected throughout the day. I can remember almost wiping things out while mowing because I wanted to text. So funny! As I cut grass on my zero-turn mower, I hoped no one videotaped me. Only a country boy texts and mows! The moment we exchanged numbers became surreal to me since I had "Amanda Gill" in my contact list through faith the whole time. I replaced (777) 777-7777 with her real phone number. I walked by faith waiting on a woman I had never met nor seen before, and now I had the ability to contact her at any given time. I randomly chose the number seven in my contact list, and later found out her favorite number is indeed seven! I believe God knew the whole time. The big things really stick out in our love story, but the little things, such as this one, happened many times. It's pretty special how God lined everything up.

Once we exchanged numbers, I asked Amanda if I could call her for the first time. She is not big on talking on the phone and would rather text. But I had to tell her everything regarding the prophecies, the wait, and what God had in store. Up to this point, she thought I was just a nice Christian guy. I knew this had to be by phone call since a text message would be insufficient giving the magnitude of the message. So that night, I went upstairs shaking like a long-tailed cat in a room full of rocking chairs! My dad sat in his recliner and I dialed her number. She answered, and for the very first time, we heard each other's voice.

After the initial greetings, I jumped right to the point at hand. In general, my personality is a no-nonsense type. I do not like to beat around the bush, and sometimes, I am regarded as blunt or too serious! It's just my personality, and I like to get things out in the open quickly. So here we go! I laid all the prophecies from my parents and myself before her. I left nothing untouched and spilled the beans in grand style. I can remember her gasping in surprise as I just leveled the conversation. As soon as I finished, we did not talk about much at all, and quickly hung up. I can remember my dad yelling from below, "Well, how did it go?" I yelled back, "Not sure!"

About that time, she messaged me. My phone beeped and we shouted for joy! My dad yelled, "Well she doesn't think you're crazy then," and we both laughed since everything now unfolded in the open. Amanda had everything to pray on, bring before the spiritual people in her life, and share with her family. I wanted everyone to know, and give God space to confirm His divine plan. I can remember Amanda telling me that she had told her dad and brother about me. Of course, I had to know what they said. She responded, "They say you could be a serial killer." I immediately thought to myself, very cool guys. If I were in their shoes, I would have probably said the same thing. We have always laughed about that, and I am glad God put everyone at ease.

But oh, how I stood confident in God. I felt like Elijah when he said pour more water on the sacrifice. I knew God watched from above, and let His glory fill the place. I did not want to hide anything, but wanted the whole world to know what God had planned. In my thinking, if it's truly God, shout it from the rooftops! The righteous are as bold as a lion, Scripture states, and this is how I felt in regards to marrying Amanda one day. People who have things to hide, and move in the shadows, should always raise a red flag within you. They move about like snakes and work in the dark to deceive. This is why I walked in boldness, and I told Amanda to let everyone important know about me. It felt amazing when I knew Amanda had private conversations with spiritual people in her life whom she truly trusted.

By now our conversations were on steroids. I had to go down to a local cell phone store and buy a smartphone. My flip phone could not handle the text messaging! I felt like Amanda faxed books over, and I telegraphed one-word responses. I tapped that flip phone to pieces basically, and knew I needed reinforcements. Being upgrade eligible, I rolled out a Cadillac of smartphones. Now I could keep up, and we were on a level playing field. We must have sent hundreds of messages throughout the day. It was like being the main actor and actress in a romantic movie that we never wanted to stop playing. We were becoming closer and had never even met yet. Is this even possible? Of course, it is! When God acts as the matchmaker, I believe the Spirit of God bears witness. Our spirits connected to one another right from the beginning. The physical realm had to hustle to catch up with the spiritual realm.

Amanda kept in close contact with her home church. Being the secretary, she had good connections with many godly people. I continued to encourage her to let them all know. I wanted everything out in the light, and I desired everyone to be in prayer on it. Amanda is a woman of faith, and I knew she followed God from the very beginning. In fact, while her prayers became more desperate, she told God before we met that she wanted to be married. Up on one of the hills near her church, late one evening, she prayed alone to God. She was ready to meet her husband and have a family of her own. Does God answer prayers? Yes, he does! On my end, God prepared me to be her husband. On the other end, God prepared Amanda to be my wife. God heard her heart's plea, and set her answer in motion. Amanda always knew that she would marry a man of God. She did not know when, but always knew in her spirit she would run alongside a preacher as they spread the gospel. Hallelujah!

From the start, I wanted Amanda to hear me preach from my home church. So, I created a private YouTube account and uploaded my sermons for her to view. As the weeks progressed, I uploaded my sermons from each Sunday service. She listened to me dissect Scripture firsthand, and one entitled "Wolves in Sheep's Clothing" became her favorite. For me, I loved sending my sermons. It sparked so many conversations about the Bible, and allowed us to connect on a spiritual level. Living so far away, I had to become creative in our relationship. Sending my sermons every week, since she could not be in attendance, helped validate my life as a preacher.

We often talked late at night, and I remember sitting in my truck to be out of the cold wind. My mom can testify: we spent hours talking. One night in particular, I sat there talking to Amanda when a car with at least four individuals pulled into our driveway. With the car idling, they just sat there with no intentions of leaving. I told Amanda, and I waited to see what they were going to do. They kept looking at the house and talking amongst themselves. Time seemed to stand still, but they were there for a good five minutes. I knew they were most likely part of an occult since we had seen many vehicles drive by real slow. Even our neighbors across the street had asked my parents at one point why there were so many vehicles parked near our house late at night.

I got tired of waiting and turned my truck on with my headlights. The car remained in the driveway, and all the people began to look my way. I put my four-wheel drive into gear, and as any country boy would do, began creeping toward them. When I got within ten feet of their car, they began slowly backing out of the driveway. I watched them pull out and drive slowly away from the house. Without a doubt, they had come to inspect the house again that night. But praise the Lord, they left and all ended well. We have had many encounters just like this one over the years. Now that Amanda and I are married, we still deal with occults, but God is continually faithful.

Welcome to My State

I used Facebook Messenger on March 24 at 8:03 p.m. to message Amanda for the first time.

About a month later, my parents and I planned our trip, loaded up the gray Honda Civic, and prepared to visit Sioux City, Iowa. That glorious morning, emotions were running high, but we were prayed up for the trip ahead. We left around three in the morning, and I remember sleeping very little in the hours prior due to all the excitement. With the GPS dialed in, and the American Flag blowing in the wind above our house, I put the car in drive and we exited the driveway.

The stars in the night sky shined brightly, and the joy in my heart bubbled over like a little boy on his birthday. I took a quick photo and sent it to Amanda even though she was sleeping. *We are on our way!* We drove onto I-57 northbound toward St. Louis, Missouri. Having my parents with me brought great comfort since I know how close they are to God. Passing the ever-famous Gateway Arch toward Kings Highway, we drove toward Kansas City, Missouri. And you guessed it, we drove without stopping until we needed fuel. We did grab a bite to eat after fueling up at a fast food restaurant. But with all the adrenaline pumping, I could barely even eat. I just wanted to arrive in the northern destination of Sioux City.

As we traveled, my parents prayed about Amanda and I drove. I remember finally seeing the "Welcome to Iowa" sign. We had never been to Iowa before, have not traveled much, and knowing we were at least in the same state made me shout for joy! In my mind, we were travelling to a distant land! We drove down I-29, and I can remember the last hour being the longest. My mom, being all crunched up with the luggage in the back seat, longed to be out of the car. Surrounded by cornfields, we pushed to see civilization!

I remember traveling up the highway and hitting potholes that shook our little car to its frame. Those potholes were more like craters from another world! It became a game as we wondered who would see the next pothole first. Once we arrived in Sioux City, we exited the off ramp and drove straight to the hotel. Stepping onto that concrete parking lot felt really good, and we stretched our legs out from the long trip. Being in basketball shorts and flip-flops, I scurried into the hotel. Maybe Amanda had lookouts, and I did not want to appear as a bum in my pajamas!

Being country folks from a small town, we have not traveled much. For those who travel all the time, a ten-hour drive is probably not that long. But to us, it became quite the endeavor! We checked into the hotel, unloaded our luggage, and exited the elevator to our second-floor room. Amanda would be picking me up in about two hours, so it gave me time to gather myself. I rested on the bed, took a shower, and waited for her arrival. As time drew near, my mom and I shared the mirror as we both got ready. It was like living at home all over again!

I remember asking my dad, "Should I hug her or shake her hand when I step into the vehicle?" First impressions are everything, and I wanted our first moment to be special.

Amanda texted me and said she was a few minutes away. I left the hotel room and headed down to the lobby. I remember her Jeep pulling into the parking lot as I stepped through the front entrance. With enough cologne on to last a week, I opened the passenger door and stepped inside. In that moment, I decided not to lean in for a hug. I instead said, "Hi there, nice to meet you" as we gave each other a firm handshake. With smiles on our faces, we pulled out of the parking lot and drove toward the mall area. Being in close proximity to the woman I had waited so long for truly gave me goosebumps. We would be meeting our parents at Red Lobster within the hour for dinner so we headed toward the mall until then.

I can remember buying Amanda a drink of her choice, a chai tea with almond milk, as we casually talked about life in Sioux City. Since the city is much bigger than my hometown, all the different areas in the mall offered many talking points. Being we were both a little tense, it helped break the ice by keeping the conversation moving. The initial eye contact, the pace in which we walked, our unique mannerisms, were all fun experiences in our first impressions of each other.

At Red Lobster, we all met each other! Our waiter sat us down at the table, and Amanda's parents came in fashionably late a few minutes later. Mike appeared exactly as I had seen in the vision, and his energy filled the room. I remember staring at him and thinking, "Wow, God really is good at descriptive intel!" The best surveillance systems in the world cannot match God! He not only sees the physical world but the inner beings of people as well. To see a man years prior in a vision, and then eat dinner with him, really is an experience like no other.

While taking our order, our waiter said, "So what brings everyone here today?" and Mike in a loud, confident answer responded, "God!" This brought the table to laughter, broke the ice, and we all joined in conversation. God had to be smiling as we all sat at the same table. I tipped the waiter thirty dollars, and Mike graciously paid for everyone's meal. What a great time, and I will always remember those first precious moments. As we exited the restaurant, I opened Amanda's door for the very first time. Country boys know how to properly open a lady's door!

We stayed a few days in Sioux City, and I spent every moment learning everything I could about her. We walked around the track at Bacon Creek, which is a scenic pond surrounded by beautiful hills and woods. Amanda loved this beautiful place, and has jogged many miles around the pond for exercise while in the military. Stopping along the way for photos, taking fun online questionnaire tests to show compatibility, and seeing Amanda laugh and smile made me forget about the world. We were lost in the moment, and the connection between us sparked like a flaming fire.

Being by Amanda's side made all the years of waiting worthwhile. All the loneliness, tears, struggles, and attacks truly disappeared into a distant memory. The next chapter of life had begun, and God had indeed authored the manuscript. While driving up and down the streets of Sioux City and taking in all the sites, I quickly learned my way around. We visited her grandparents often, hung out with her good friend Saundra, met her sister Micah for lattes at a local coffee shop, joined Gabriel for dinner, and spent much time with Amanda's loved ones. They were excited to finally meet the man from southern Illinois, and I enjoyed getting to know them as well.

I vividly remember Grandma Jeanne giving me the biggest hug in the world, and told me if I needed a good Christian woman, I had indeed found her. She spoke very highly of Amanda and the life that she lived for God. Well hallelujah, I love when others speak about one's relationship with Christ! Amanda's family and friends opened their arms wide, and showed my parents and me great hospitality while we visited. The first time in Sioux City will forever be etched in my memory, and experiencing a prophecy fulfilled is truly a bigger-than-life moment.

The big elephant in the room that could not go unnoticed was: Is this the real Amanda Gill? I awaited confirmation while we were there. One afternoon, while we walked around Bacon Creek, God dropped in my spirit that she was indeed the one I would marry. I told her that very day with full confidence on one of the park benches. Of course, she moved with caution for it takes time for something of that magnitude to sink in! That night at the hotel room, I received further confirmation from the two most influential people in my life. Once I told my parents Amanda was the one, my mom said God told her before we even left for Sioux City. While cleaning the house, God dropped the news into her spirit. She did not say a word to me before we left because she waited to see if God would tell me directly. Then to bring further confirmation to my family, my dad had an open vision in the hotel room where we were staying. My dad sat in a chair in the corner of the room, and in the vision, Jesus appeared with a smile on His face. With all three of us knowing in the spirit, it put everyone at ease. I wasn't just some random guy coming after Amanda. God had led me to Sioux City, Iowa, in direct obedience. If it had not been for God, and the leading of my pastors, we would have never even crossed paths.

While attending church on Sunday, a funny moment happened when Amanda and I drove up the hill to our parking spot. As she put the vehicle in park, she covered her calves with her long dress. I wondered exactly why she laughed and covered them up so quickly. She looked right at me and said, "Don't look, I haven't shaved in a few days!" I laughed out loud, but I loved the funny side of her cute personality. Amanda is so genuine, and I knew from that little moment she cared about what I thought of her appearance. She liked me, and I could tell. Before she grabbed the door handle, I remember shouting, "Wait!" I quickly exited and walked around the vehicle to open her door. I later found out that some of Amanda's family were watching from inside the church, and were impressed with how I treated Amanda from the beginning. And even today, I open Amanda's door at every opportunity. Chivalry in this country needs to come back, and women need to be back on the pedestal.

Years prior, before Amanda even knew I existed, I bought gifts for her to show my faith in God. I mentioned a list of items earlier in the book. Having saved the best for last, I have to tell you the story behind a handmade necklace. My sister Shannon and I were out shopping one day for a Christmas gift for Amanda. It was in December, and I remember it being really cold outside that day with snow still on the ground. While shopping at a local jewelry store off Route 13 in a small town called Carterville, she began to tell me of a girl she knew who was the daughter of one of her co-workers. This girl made engraved necklaces for extra money while in school, and had really showcased her work online. Shannon showed me some photos of the things she had created, and I thought it would be really nice to have one made for Amanda. I ordered the necklace with the engraved inscription "A perfect match made in Heaven" on the first pendant and "b.e.+a.e.=love" on the smaller pendant. The two pendants hung on a chain necklace with pink and turquoise beads hanging down.

One morning when Amanda picked me up at the hotel, I presented the necklace to Amanda. She smiled as she opened the box, especially when she read the inscription. She absolutely loved the necklace, and the story behind it blew her away. Having wiped dust off that little gray box for all those years, seeing the necklace on Amanda skyrocketed my faith in God. He led me right to Amanda, and knew the whole time we would be husband and wife one day.

One thing that began to change quickly upon meeting Amanda was the beverages and food that I consumed. Amanda is "Mrs. Organic" and enjoys healthy foods. She views our bodies as the temples of God, and wants to care for herself in order to please Him. She loves buying minimally processed foods, and while we were in Sioux City, she would take me into local grocery stores to purchase healthy snacks and drinks. Like kale chips, roasted seaweed, dried mangos, raw sushi, live culture yogurts, spinach smoothies, and coconut milk—and this is just tipping the iceberg! I always thought I ate fairly healthy for a country boy, but things began to slowly change as we embarked on our relationship. No more soda, for one! I haven't had a soda in about five years thanks to Amanda. With all the sugar and bad ingredients, she convinced me to stop. Instead, she started buying me healthy items that I had never even heard of in my life!

Even now as a family, we grow a garden, buy organic foods, and try to eat healthy to the best of our abilities. We do splurge sometimes for ice cream or fast food, though! As I think back, I remember traveling up Gordon Drive with the windows down, drinking organic teas, while headed to Amanda's church on the hill. Those summer days with my girl will always hold a special place in my heart.

My birthday is April 26. My first in-person interaction with Amanda happened on the weekend of my birthday. God gave me the best birthday gift of my life. The time flew by quickly, but our relationship grew at a rapid rate as well. To experience authentic prophecies is a real faith booster, and it is something that most people think only happened in the Bible. We lived it, though, and reality eventually caught up with the spiritual realm. On April 27, after only staying a few days, we packed to head home. I can remember leaving the hotel very early. But I had one last thing to do before we left.

In faith, over those four years, I bought Amanda many gifts. I put my faith in action while trusting God for a woman whom I had never even met. I had bags of lotions, perfumes, and body sprays that I had bought for her. With only limited time to present all the gifts, I held some of them back for a special cause. I had an idea of leaving the rest of the gifts at her house. As we pulled up in the middle of the night, I jogged up the hill to lay them on her front porch! As I scurried across the lawn, I hoped no one saw a man figure moving past the windows. I did not want her dad thinking an ill-intentioned man crept outside his house. That could have turned into a funny story later on, but wouldn't have been one then! I tiptoed back to the car, quietly shut the door, and we headed back to southern Illinois. After a few hours, I called and told Amanda to check the front porch. Underneath the little bench, all the gifts in their original bags awaited. I can still remember the excitement in her voice! Such joy filled my heart. To be honest, it became the highlight of the drive home.

After waiting all those years for Amanda, putting miles between us again, really sunk my heart. But I knew it would only be temporary until I saw her again. We finally reached West Frankfort, and I can remember slowing up on Interstate 57 to take a photo of the green "Welcome to West Frankfort" sign. I texted Amanda the photo, and told her it would be an excellent place for her to visit.

On May 27, Amanda listened to my advice! She planned a trip to visit southern Illinois. I can remember picking her up at Lambert airport in St. Louis. While sitting in my parents' Honda Civic in a parking lot near the runway, I watched the flight information screen for her arrival time to appear. With multiple planes landing from different directions, I had no idea which plane had my sweetheart on board. It was around ten o' clock that evening, and the moon and stars were shining brightly. As I watched the sky for planes from the Iowa direction, my phone vibrated and she texted, "just landed." I quickly drove to the pickup spot and waited to see her through the large lobby windows.

With a dozen freshly cut red roses in hand, I stepped out of the car when I saw her and exchanged the bouquet for her luggage! This time, I hugged her instead of shaking her hand! With smiles on both of our faces, we loaded her luggage in the trunk and headed toward West Frankfort. One thing for sure, she packed one big military-style suitcase. I went to hoist it in the trunk, and it felt like half her closet made the trip. Being her first time in St. Louis, she enjoyed all the lights of the city. In route to Interstate 57, we headed to a Quality Inn in Marion, Illinois. I chose this hotel in particular for Amanda while visiting since I thought it was one of the safest places for the price point. Since I am naturally a security guy, making sure Amanda had a safe visit landed near the top of my priority list. The hotel is well trafficked, surrounded by lights, and has nice restaurants around it—and being only ten minutes from my parents' house, it fit the bill.

We seized the days while Amanda visited for the first time. I had our dates planned, of course, and tried to showcase southern Illinois with all the beautiful rural areas. One of the first things on our adventure list included horseback riding in the Shawnee National Forest. I paid to have a trail guide take us through the woodlands, which really displayed the scenic beauty of our region. While we rode our horses through an open field, a beautiful Monarch butterfly landed on Amanda's arm. I told her not to move! I quickly grabbed my phone and captured the moment.

We both rode bay horses that were really broke, but I prayed to God at the beginning of the trails, please do not let her get bucked off! Being around horses my whole life, I know even a good horse can have a bad day. As we stopped later on an open trail, we posed for another photo, and our horses touched noses as if they were kissing. Our trail guide caught the image, and we will forever cherish that moment. That photo now sits on my nightstand next to my side of the bed!

A beautiful place to visit as well is Paducah, Kentucky, which is about a forty-five-minute drive south of my parents' home. We planned a day with my sister, Shannon, and her husband, Mark. While there, we ate a fine steak dinner along the river and took a horse-drawn carriage ride through the old brick streets of the downtown area. Beautiful weather, an amazing girl, and the atmosphere became electric as we sat along the banks of the Ohio River. Sitting on those large river rocks as a slight breeze came off the water, Amanda and I enjoyed the romantic scenery together. As we talked about many things, the tugboats began disappearing into the night, and the stars glistened over our lovely evening. On the drive home, as we crossed back over state lines, I told Amanda southern Illinois would be a great place to live. She gave me one of those big smiles as she imagined living with me in southern Illinois.

Amanda not only spent time with me, but she also began building her lifelong relationships with my family. We had cookouts with barbeque ribs and cooked s'mores on bonfires, and as we sat around the old firepit, I recalled the words of God long ago: "Stay here and don't move, and I will bring you a wife." With my feet propped up on the same rocks, I knew God had to be well pleased.

Amanda loves movies and popcorn! So, the next evening, we headed to a local theater to enjoy one of her favorite pastimes. On the highway, I could tell Amanda thought on something because her eyes were fixed as she stared out the passenger window. We pulled into the parking lot, and being how I like everything out in the open, I asked her to tell me. With a smile on her face, she asked me to be her boyfriend. So, on May 30 of year 2015, Amanda and I became boyfriend and girlfriend, officially. We could now change our status on Facebook to "In a relationship"! Words cannot describe how excited we were, and even more so, as we just knew God had to be smiling from above. Later that evening, before I dropped Amanda off at the hotel, I wrote "A+B" with a giant heart around it on the inside of my truck's driver's side window. I used my index finger to draw on the condensation that had formed on the glass. Even months later, on cold nights, it would reappear because I never washed that section of my window! I wanted that original heart drawing to last indefinitely.

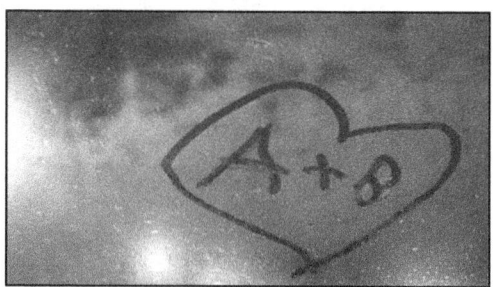

As Amanda's first visit came to an end, just to further add validity to the story, I showed her the crinkled-up gift receipts of the items purchased for her before we ever met. I kept the receipts in a fireproof lockbox to show the dates.

As we drove to St. Louis, she wore the silver pendant necklace (receipt shown above) that I had bought for her before we met. As we unloaded at the airport, and gave our good-byes, I teared up as she walked away through the terminal. Grown man crying over a woman? Indeed! I wanted to go with her badly, and never leave her side. A long-distance relationship is challenging, but as God continued to orchestrate His divine plan, we patiently trusted Him. Before I pulled out of the airport parking lot, we were already texting each other as she boarded the plane. That constant connection through communication kept our relationship growing despite all the distance between us.

While Amanda visited, I did not sleep much. I picked her up early in the mornings and dropped her off late in the evenings. And when I returned home while she visited, I was too excited about everything to truly sleep. I tossed and turned in bed until that alarm sounded. So, the drive home from the airport is the closest I have ever been to falling asleep at the wheel. I remember stopping along the interstate at a rest stop just to rest my eyes. I jumped out of the car, walked along the pavement, and tried to wake myself up. As I exited the interstate, I could not wait to crawl into bed! Once I pulled into my parents' driveway, I headed straight for my upstairs room. I slept all evening just to recuperate from that week. It's kind of like when one goes on vacation, and due to running from one thing to the next, they need a "home vacation" to rest the week they return. This is how I felt!

Through the coming weeks, Amanda and I talked for hours on the phone. We used apps like Facetime and Tango to actually see each other during our conversations. Sometimes we would talk on the phone till two or three in the morning, and then struggle to get up for work the next day. What did we do the whole time? We would read the Bible to each other, talk about our childhoods, talk about our families, discuss favorite foods—all the "get to know you better" things.

One topic that helped us once we were married involved our understanding of our individual needs in our relationship. Figuring out what made us feel loved, and vice versa, what made us not feel loved, did wonders in our relationship. Being brutally honest with each other established the framework for our maturation as a couple. For example, Amanda really enjoys spending time together. It does not have to be an expensive outing or some luxurious vacation, but she needs that connection between her and me. Even as of today, one of our favorite pastimes is spending quality time with each other while sitting at a local coffee shop. We love dropping the kiddos off at my parents to order lattes and engage in conversation. Watching the cars go by, observing people going to and fro, and smelling the fresh aroma of coffee beans sure makes for a lovely Saturday afternoon.

In our late-night conversations, we agreed on taking spiritual action in our relationship by fasting from food together. As a couple, we wanted God's will above all else. We abstained from food to connect ourselves with our Lord and Savior. Fasting is a mighty tool used throughout Scripture to move us closer to Him. We still exercise this spiritual tool in our marriage today. It is mighty in tearing down strongholds!

Crash on the Hill

One late summer evening, Amanda did not respond to my texts nor my phone calls. I remember telling my dad something had to be wrong. I laid in the upstairs loft praying for Amanda, and wondering why she did not answer back. Had I said something that upset her or did something serious happen? As I lay awake in my bed around midnight, I could hear my dad ease into his recliner as he always does to pray. My dad heard me upstairs, and from below asked if I had heard from Amanda yet. I told him no and asked him to pray. I am guessing around two in the morning, Amanda finally texted. She told me that something had happened, and she would fill me in with all the details in the morning. It left me hanging, but seeing her texts at least allowed me to sleep.

The next morning, her brother Gabriel called me from his workplace. He told me that Amanda had been in a car crash at the bottom of a hill near her church. As I stepped onto the front porch of the house, my heart raced with the sudden news of the accident. All the thoughts associated with a loved one being in a wreck filled my mind. He said that Amanda passed out before impact, and paramedics drove her to the emergency room. She had a pierced lung, a fractured rib, and bruises all over her face. Oh, my goodness! I called her sister Micah, and she filled me in more with all the details.

Amanda had decided to head to church that evening to catch up on some last-minute tasks that needed to be done. Being a secretary at the church, Amanda had to meet deadlines and make sure everything ran smoothly for the upcoming services. Upon leaving the gym after a workout, she traveled down the interstate and had pains in her stomach that caused extreme discomfort. As she exited onto the off ramp toward the church, the pains intensified as she tried to seek relief by repositioning herself in the seat. Roughly a quarter mile away from her turn-off, she completely passed out on the highway. Driving at least 55 mph, her Jeep miraculously stayed on course until she reached the bottom of her church's driveway. As the Jeep began to veer off the road, Amanda remained unconscious, and the Jeep hit a tree and totaled on impact. The tree actually kept her from flying over the hill into a deep ravine, and thank goodness, the seatbelt kept her from propelling through the windshield.

A passing car stopped immediately and two gentlemen ran to her aid. They called 911, and paramedics arrived shortly thereafter. In their witness of the account, they said Amanda's Jeep had become airborne at one point as it gained speed before impact. As shattered glass and vehicle parts laid all around, Amanda regained consciousness as first responders pulled her out of the mangled Jeep. Paramedics rushed her to the hospital by ambulance and notified her father, Mike. Within minutes he arrived at the emergency room, and he stayed by Amanda's side the whole time. The wreck could have been much worse, and thank goodness no other people were involved in the accident. We never knew the medical cause of the pain, but we rebuked the devil and praised God for guardian angels!

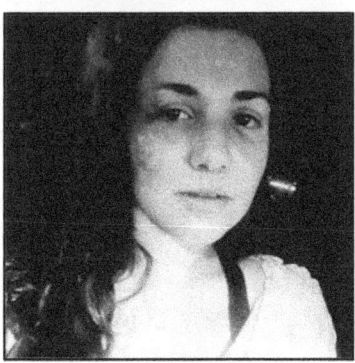

I remember Amanda sending me hospital photos of herself, and I felt helpless while being so far away. The bruises under her eyes told the story of the air bag releasing on impact. She stayed at home the next few weeks by doctor orders to let her body recuperate. And of course, wanting to see her soon, I moved my trip back to Sioux City up on the calendar. I left early in the morning a few days later and hit the road by myself like a pheasant out of the brush. My parents could not make the trip this time. The long trip gave me a lot of time to pray! About forty-five minutes from Sioux City, I pulled over to change my clothes at the rest stop. Leaving in pajamas for comfort on the trip, I did not want to show up like a scrub. I changed my clothes in the car, fixed my hair, brushed my teeth, applied deodorant and cologne, and trimmed my beard so I would look presentable.

I headed straight for Amanda's house and arrived around 1 p.m. One of the first things we did included visiting the hill of the crash. Being Amanda moved slowly from soreness, I had to help her out of the car. The tire tracks from her Jeep were still there, and the little tree looked like it had been hit by a Mack truck. As we stood by the tree overlooking the embankment, I thanked God for keeping my sweetheart safe. Despite a few things that needed a little time to heal, Amanda came out very well. I believe the devil had tried to interrupt God's plan, but with all my prayers of protection over Amanda, his plan failed.

As I returned back home from seeing Amanda after the wreck, I spent a lot of time in prayer. Amanda and I had met, but I would not put God on the back burner.

Even though the prophecies were unfolding, I knew how crucial my close relationship with God had to be. I used to sit on an old twelve-foot trailer with headphones on and worship God with all my might. I blessed him with my worship, and I felt His presence as I rocked back and forth on that old trailer. God speaks to us anywhere, whether inside or outside. It can be a very busy day or a slow, rainy evening. It can be in pajamas or in a seven-piece suit. Does not matter if a believer truly knows when the Shepherd speaks.

One day, as I worshipped God, He told me, "Tell Amanda that she will fall in love with you." I waited a few days, but then one evening I dialed her number. As she sat on a picnic table with her brother Gabriel, she picked up the phone. We talked briefly as Gabriel headed into the house. As I had done since day one, I just leveled the conversation again, and said, "God told me to tell you that you will fall in love with me." An awkward thing to say, but I had to let it fly! In the coming weeks, we continued to text and call each other nonstop. We would sometimes talk on the phone till three or four in the morning. The divine connection that we shared made us fall deeper in love with every passing moment.

Just for the record, I did tell Amanda that I loved her first. Even till this day, I always tell her that I loved her first, which means I love her more since I have been loving her longer than she has loved me. A tongue-twister sentence, but all truth! She always disagrees, and it is a cute thing between us. I always tell her that one day when she makes it to Heaven, God will finally confirm to her this truth. She just smiles and says, "Nope!"

On Bended Knee

As our love kindled like a hot oak fire, I always told Amanda that I would have married her the first time we met in Sioux City. Of course, she needed time to pray and think on these things! I came into her life on a direct command from God, and for Amanda, she walked out the divine miracle day by day. She fell in love with me as God had said, and her life would be turned upside down in the days ahead.

In the one-horse towns of southern Illinois, I began shopping for the perfect wedding ring. I saved close to five thousand dollars to buy the prettiest array of diamonds I could find. I knew Amanda would wear this ring for the rest of her life, and I wanted the very best for her. I shopped all around the area, and eventually found one at a local family-owned jeweler in Carbondale. The ring consists of rose gold, has a matching wedding band, and has the most beautiful arrangement of diamonds. I remember being in the store for hours, just to make sure the ring met my requirements for my lovely bride to be. I bought the lifetime warranty, for this is how I view our relationship, and walked out the door with ring in hand. When I returned home, I remember showing my mom the ring in the lights of their kitchen.

The ring sparkled with the bright lights shining down on it. My mom loved the ring, and thought the rose gold had a unique look that separated it from other rings. With the engagement ring finally in hand, I began to plan my proposal to Amanda, and scheduled my next trip to Iowa. Before heading up, I contacted Mike and talked with him on the phone. I asked his permission to marry Amanda, and he told me that I had truly swept Amanda off her feet. He said "yes," and God's plan became one step closer to fruition. Amanda had a heads-up on what I asked Mike, though, as she sat in the dining room during our conversation. It's kind of hard to completely surprise someone from such a far distance! We had only been talking since March, and only a few months down the road, I prepared myself to ask Amanda to be my wife.

This rose gold engagement ring would replace her purity ring, and symbolize our covenant to be married. Thoughts on where I should propose, how I should ask the big question, what I should wear, and all the little details flooded my mind. I am a planner by nature, and I desired fireworks for Amanda.

On July 22, I headed up to see my sweetheart. With the engagement ring nestled tight in my luggage, I could not wait to propose. I chose a hill at Bacon Creek to propose, and with a bench facing the sunset across the lake, I thought the view would be lovely. I can remember driving to the spot on July 24, and stepping out of the car to open Amanda's door. I hid the ring in my sock, and had it positioned so I could grab it in a smooth fashion. The sun shined brightly, the water glimmered through the openings between the trees, and a fresh breeze swept across the parking lot. What a perfect day! I wish I could say she had no idea, but after she overheard the conversation with her dad a few nights earlier, she expected the proposal.

As we walked up the hill toward the bench, I simply could not wait any longer. I mean, come on! After waiting almost four years, I just could not bring myself to continue walking up that hill without a ring on her finger. I quickly sent the plan of proposing on the bench right out the door, and on that narrow uphill walkway, I dropped to one knee. As I grabbed Amanda's hand, I asked her to marry me and be my wife. She gleamed as she stared at the ring and said, "YES!" It became official now! We were engaged, and I can remember hugging Amanda as we were caught up in the amazing moment. We were living a dream that only God could give.

I called home to let my family know. We began telling her loved ones, and we embraced being soon-to-be newlyweds! We were engaged almost four months after our initial contact. When God is on the move, one has to be ready to run with Him. I never dreamed we would meet on Facebook, I never knew we would be engaged so quickly, and with all the negative stigma surrounding long-distance relationships, I never thought God would connect two people who lived so far away from each other. But God is number one in relationships, and He does what He wants.

Amanda always thought she would date the "one" for a couple years before engagement, but when God confirmed to her about me, she had no hesitation. Always remember, God is not on our time frame; we are on His. Sometimes, we have to patiently wait for years for His plan to unfold. On other occasions and especially in our love story, we have to run to catch up with Him. We always laugh too about how I proposed on the walkway. It is a reflection of my no-nonsense, do-things-very-quickly personality. I just could not wait any longer! It became like an out-of-body experience when she said, "YES!"

Wedding Bells Ringing

Our wonderful friend Saundra wanted to do our engagement photos for us, free of charge. Amanda and Saundra had met in fourth grade, and have been good friends since then. We ended up picking like the hottest day of the year for our photos. As a kid on a farm, we baled hay for the horses every summer. It is hot, itchy, and not for the weak. This day reminded me of those long summer days in the fields. Nearing one hundred degrees, we walked through Bacon Creek as we posed for "cute" photos. With our wedding day being planned, we had a wonderful time capturing the surreal moment. Amanda is very photogenic, but I am on the opposite spectrum. She has actually taught me over the years to be more photogenic, and has shown me how a country boy should correctly pose for photos. We took some at Bacon Creek, then an old abandoned warehouse in the downtown area, and then topped it off on the hills near her church. With my ring on Amanda's finger now, the dream had become reality.

Amanda and I both lived with our parents. We chose January 2, 2016 for the wedding date. What a way to start the new year! With all the excitement building, we had absolutely no place to live. So, when I returned home, I began looking for houses. I could not bring my gorgeous bride to southern Illinois to live in my parents' attic! I would have needed to fast and pray myself through if God desired it to be that way. Thanks be to God for allowing me to finally move out and look for a place for two newlyweds.

My parents and I drove around neighboring towns looking for houses up for sale. I would look online as well, but we couldn't find anything we liked or fit our budget. Amanda and I talked about what we wanted, but time continued to tick by. We only had a few months to find and close on a home. We prayed for the right one. Then one day when I scanned the internet, a new listing appeared. A small house that offered nothing special but met initial requirements of needing a place to stay. I contacted a realtor friend, and we scheduled a walk-through of the home. My parents and I loved it. It had only two bedrooms, and needed some tender and loving care, but it priced below our price point and had tremendous potential. I told our realtor that we wanted it, and she began to negotiate the price. We agreed with the seller on final closing statements, and the process to close began. Roughly thirty days later, on October 15, I had keys to our first home.

It was a fixer-upper to say the least, so I began working on the house immediately. I slept on an old military cot for weeks as I remodeled the entire inside of the home. My parents and I painted all the walls, installed new hardwood floors, bought new appliances, landscaped the outside, put up new blinds, and really put in the work to make our first home special. I sent Amanda photos of our progress, and she chimed in on the interior decorating. The place slowly but surely became ready to be inhabited by two people deeply in love!

With our wedding date approaching quickly, Amanda planned on coming down in November to see the house. We had to somehow manage to move all her belongings to southern Illinois. Mike and Gayle rented a U-Haul for us, and they loaded all her belongings like a can of sardines. Amanda has so many things, a small miracle occurred when the door closed on the moving truck! From the floor to the ceiling, they could not fit one more item. On November 13, my parents and I met Amanda halfway, just outside of Kansas City, Missouri. At the gas station, we pulled up next to her, and I jumped into the driver's seat. We were on our way to southern Illinois with the official move. We met in March and now in November, we were moving Amanda's things to our new house in preparation for the wedding.

I remember walking Amanda through our home for the first time, and showing her all the improvements. I anxiously waited for her "I love it" approval as we toured the house. Being our first little home, we began setting things up in the house. We decorated, moved things around, cleaned, and Amanda put her artistic touches on the place. Like always, before I returned home at night, I made sure the doors were locked before I left. For a few nights, before traveling back to Sioux City, Amanda stayed at the house that would be our dwelling for a couple years. In that same week, we used her military discount to purchase a new Honda Accord so we would have a family vehicle. Everything happened so fast! But with the long-awaited wedding just around the corner, preparation for the big day had to take place.

Have you ever planned a wedding? Wow! It is like a hurricane. Booking the photographer, choosing the catering company, picking songs for the reception, color coordinating outfits, buying flowers, buying wedding bands, tasting cakes, having my family travel to Iowa, and so much more! As a man, I just let Amanda do her thing! The colors of our wedding were white, blue, silver, and black. With help from Micah and Saundra, the planning of the wedding happened without any mishaps. Amanda desired a large wedding, and due to Mike's gracious blessing, we had one that we will always remember.

> "Therefore, shall a man leave his father and his mother, and shall cleave unto his wife: and they shall be one flesh." – Genesis 2:24

What an incredible day on January 2, 2016. Emotions were high and the hours ahead changed our lives forever. On the hills of Sioux City, the sun glistened on top of the fresh white snow. I remember walking through the snow in my dress shoes as it crackled underneath to help our photographer capture the beautiful landscape. The wind in Iowa is fierce, and it penetrates all clothing, especially dress pants. Like wow! I recall the sun shining brightly, but the bitter cold froze everything, including the entire wedding party. The bridesmaids were trying not to shake as they stepped outside in the ungodly cold air. As they huddled around, the photographer positioned them to capture the moment. As I watched everything unfold, I stood in awe of God, who had made it all come to pass. From the firepit area at my parents' to standing in the snow with the bridal party, God had surpassed my wildest expectations.

As I anticipated seeing my beautiful bride for the first time, our photographer sent Micah to lead me to the spot. With eyes closed, I stood there listening to Amanda walk up from the opposite direction. Standing back to back, our photographer steadied to capture the moment where we saw each other for the first time on our big day. I can remember anticipating what Amanda would look like, but as I turned, my eyes beheld beauty on a scale only made for angels. Amanda looked breathtaking, and her beauty accompanied by her big smile made me one happy man.

Being as we had never kissed; I could not wait to stand up on the altar to kiss her on the lips for the first time. I could not wait for her to wear my ring forever. I could not wait for Amanda to be my wife. I could not wait to spend every waking moment with the woman God had truly picked for my life. With great excitement, we were living the prophecy. From our first Facebook message, ten months later we were walking in wedding bliss.

God had indeed performed His promise to Amanda and me. With Him, we celebrated the beginning of the best days of our lives. Standing on the altar, we had such a beautiful ceremony that incorporated our firm beliefs in the Word of God. As everyone watched, Amanda and I dedicated ourselves to each other. We were committed to God first, and vowed to please Him with a strong marriage. It is a vow that will stand the test of time for those who remain committed to Him. We sealed everything with our first kiss, as we were introduced as "Mr. and Mrs. Emery." We stepped down from the altar and made our way through the crowd to celebrate the goodness of God Almighty. Driving down the hill, we were husband and wife! I love Amanda and have the opportunity to show her my love all my days. How awesome is God? He orchestrated a perfect plan.

Our reception immediately proceeded our wedding, and we held the celebration at Stony Creek Hotel. The music, the guests, the catered food, and all the decorations made the evening one to remember. We celebrated a wonderful Christian wedding orchestrated by God.

Amanda ended up shoving cake in my face, which she is still repenting over! Being on cloud nine, I embraced the cake and frosting. We danced to our first wedding song and goofed around with our families, and it will forever be branded in our memories. The next morning, we drove to the Ozark Mountains of Missouri to spend our honeymoon together. My parents accommodated our trip, and special thanks to them for blessing us financially on our first week together.

Amanda and I had abstained from sex until after our marriage covenant. We waited to please the Lord, and did not desecrate His Word. Walking according to God's standards is how one remains in good standing. With all He has done for us, we strive to please Him in every aspect of our lives. Our love for Him pushes us to obey Him.

> "If ye love me, keep my commandments." – John 14:15

A Happy Family

Within the last four years of our marriage, we have been incredibly blessed. We now have three amazing kiddos, and our family is still nestled in the palms of God's mighty hands. Our first born is Amiyah Louise Emery, who we welcomed into the world on March 3, 2017; secondly is Silas Michael Emery, who came into our lives on July 5, 2018; and just recently, Ezra Dean Emery joined them on October 11, 2019. Married in 2016, and now in 2020, we still remember all God has done. Life moves quickly, but I can still remember my first time in Sioux City while driving up Gordon Drive. We rolled the windows down, listened to music, and drank organic teas. And now as my beautiful wife, and the mother of our three little blessings, I love her more today than I did then.

We spent the first two years of our marriage in our little house in Herrin, Illinois. I scurried to find one for us to live in, and had little time to choose! I had to fix it up as I mentioned before, but we were quickly outgrowing that cozy place. Amanda began to look for a house. One of the credentials is it had to be in close proximity to my parents. We drove around areas looking for potential homes on the weekend. We had a few walk-through visits, but nothing ever seemed to work. Then one night, while visiting my parents, I walked into my dad's study. We began to shoot the breeze about homes, and I told him that we really needed to find something. We had our little girl Amiyah, and were expecting Silas soon. When all of a sudden, my dad said, "We are thinking about selling this one maybe next year." The lightbulb went off! I said, "Why don't you sell it to us, and we can just add on?"

Well the next day, we settled on a price! We contacted a contractor, and everything began to work perfectly. Our new bedroom now sits in the exact spot where I prayed for Amanda. I prayed many nights on that old deck, and now our bedroom sits on that piece of ground. I cannot tell you how many nights I looked up at the stars on that old deck praying for a woman I had never even met. The chicken pens my dad and I built are now used by Amiyah in collecting eggs, and we still have the white rock bantam chickens. In the summer of year 2011, I had sat motionless by the firepit. God said, "Stay here, and don't move, and I will bring you a wife." He sure did.

Tips for Single Christians

Do not try and copy exactly what God did in our lives. If God is not in it, then you will fall flat on your face! We had a man not too long ago try this very thing. He became caught up in his emotions, started prophesying from his own desires, bought gifts, and told everyone that he would be marrying a woman. The woman basically thought he had gone mad, and wanted nothing to do with him. This is not a "Do these seven steps and it will happen to you" kind of a book. We told our story to illustrate how mightily God can work when He is given free rein to do His will. Yes, God can put you together with someone if it lines up with His will. It is indeed a narrow walk, takes great faith, but if He can do it for us, He can do it for you.

Follow God and not your heart. Emotions and feelings will lie to you. The worldly way of doing things is to "follow your heart." But as Christians, we need to follow God, and not become wrapped up in a whirlwind of emotions and youthful lusts. Stay in the Word, learn God's voice, submit to a godly pastor, remain out of sin, and work on growing into spiritual maturity while you wait for your companion. Be wise and save yourself much heartache by following your inner spirit, which is connected to a holy God, and not your heart.

For men and women alike, stay away from pornography. This alluring temptation ruins marriages, and even if you're single, the sin will carry over into your marriage one day. It is an addiction just like heroine, meth, or cocaine. Lusting for things through a screen is the devil's way of keeping you in a fantasy world of filth that will eventually send you to Hell if you do not repent. The Bible explains it very well!

> "But I say unto you, that whosoever looketh on a woman to lust after her hath committed adultery with her already in his heart." – Matthew 5:28

Whether in person or through a screen, the Bible says if you lust after someone with sexual intentions then you have committed adultery within the heart. To be pleasing to God, you have to remain pure within your mind. This applies to a single individual or one who is in a marriage covenant. It takes work and dedication to remain pure within the theater of the mind. But again, God sees you even behind closed doors. If you want to be blessed by God, then you need to strive to be holy in all you do. Stay away from the short-term sexual satisfactions that will leave you void, and prepare for marriage where the bed is undefiled. God created sex to draw a couple closer in physical intimacy, and to promote replenishing the earth with children. Sex is a wonderful and beautiful thing—do not mess it up. Do it His way!

For the single men out there, do not fall for the "damsel in distress" scenario. Just because a woman needs someone to rescue her does not mean you are the chosen knight. Christian men often try to help a woman, even if it's an ungodly woman unfortunately, and swoop in to save the day. This will only delay time and open doors for sin. In addition, dating a woman who is not a strong possibility for marriage is a complete waste of time. If you cannot see yourself with the woman for the rest of your life, do not swoop in and begin playing with her emotions. It is much easier to stay away from a relationship than it is to get out of one. If the woman does not meet Christian standards outlined in the Bible, let the idea of courting her fly away like a balloon in the wind. She is not ready to be a wife, and you are wasting your precious time.

Instead, look for a woman who has integrity. For example, if a woman dresses skimpily like Jezebel, then she is most likely walking in lasciviousness, and definitely not ready for a serious relationship. She desires your attention in a very ungodly way. Women who love God with all their heart strive to please God in every aspect of their lives. A woman can still dress attractive without compromising her self-worth. In the book of Proverbs, we find what God thinks of a virtuous woman.

"Who can find a virtuous woman? For
her price is far above rubies." – Proverbs
31:10

The search is long and the price is expensive. In
short, look for a woman whom you would see meeting
this high honor of being called virtuous. Once you find
her, pray on the matter, seek advice from your pastor,
and wait until you know God's will. If all checks out
initially, still proceed with caution. Marriage is indeed
intended to be one life commitment.

For you married men out there, you have survived
reading this book up until now! Way to go, brothers. I
am going to drop an atomic word bomb on you right
now, though. We are commanded to love our wives as
Christ did the church. You will stand before God
someday and give account on how you loved your wife.

"Husbands, love your wives, even as
Christ also loved the church, and gave
himself for it." – Ephesians 5:25

Jesus died for the church and we are supposed to
love our wives with that same zeal and passion! Does
not matter if you have been married six months or sixty
years; love her to the best of your ability all your days. If
you are single, be prepared to meet this high standard.

It's your turn, ladies! Do not think that you will just
"fix" the man. So many women fall into this trap. The
man will start going to church just to please the woman.
They will utter things like, "I think God wants us to be

together." Ungodly men often use God's name like a hashtag to try and validate their desire, but their plan has nothing to do with God. This is a prime example of spiritual fraud. Once they are married, the man will begin to drift away. If a man cannot stand on his own two feet spiritually with God now, he is not husband material. Scripture is very specific.

> "Wives, submit yourselves unto your own husbands, as unto the Lord."
> – Ephesians 5:22

If you are going to follow this command, find a man worthy of submitting to each and every day. A man needs to be in church faithfully for at least three years. In general, I think this is a good rule of thumb. In addition, watch how a man treats his mother. This is often a good indicator of how he will treat you down the road. Hold onto your integrity, and find a man who puts God above you. If he truly does put you second, you have truly found a man worth loving all your days. Hold onto him, respect him, and be blessed with a wonderful marriage.

Salvation Prayer

My great grandpa received Christ as his Savior at the very end of his life. A man that steered away from anything involving church his whole life, became radically saved. Upon salvation in his living room, He quoted these famous words to my family with tears in his eyes, "Why did I wait so long?" We baptized him in an old bathtub, and the change in his demeanor could not go unnoticed! He passed away approximately two months later. Do I believe in death bed confessions? Yes! We will one day walk the streets of gold together. But take his advice, choose to serve the King today. Tomorrow is promised to no unsaved man or woman.

> "Go to now, ye that say, today or tomorrow we will go into such a city, and continue there a year, and buy and sell, and get gain. Whereas ye know not what shall be on the morrow. For what is your life? It is even a vapour, that appeareth for a little time, and then vanisheth away." – James 4:13-14

If Jesus is not the Lord of your life right now, please say this simple prayer below with me. This decision is hands down the greatest you will ever make on earth. No matter what your past is like, God has the power to save you. Change your life today!

Lord Jesus, I repent of all my sins. I ask you to forgive me, cast my sins into the depths of the sea, and come into my life. I denounce the works of the devil, and give you full control. I believe you died for my sins, conquered Hell and the grave, and will return one day to establish your Kingdom on earth. I will turn from my past and strive to sanctify myself all of my days. Because your Word is truth, I confess by my mouth that I am saved and cleansed by your blood. In Jesus mighty name, Amen!

> "For God so loved the world, that he gave his only begotten Son, that whosoever believeth in him should not perish, but have everlasting life." – John 3:16

> "Therefore, if any man be in Christ, he is a new creature: old things are passed away; behold, all things are become new." – II Corinthians 5:17

About the Author

Brandon D. Emery holds a master's degree in Education with a concentration in Student Personnel. He is an assistant pastor at Rugged Cross Chapel in southern Illinois. As a writer, he uses his life experiences as a tool to help young single Christians further their walk with God. As his family moves in the gifts of the Holy Ghost, their church operates in sound doctrine, spiritual power, and the love of Christ.

He is happily married to his beautiful wife, Amanda L. Emery. A perfect match made in Heaven that took years for the prophetic words to finally come to pass. Together, they have three children: Amiyah L. Emery, Silas M. Emery, and Ezra D. Emery. He enjoys spending time with his family while creating long-lasting memories. Together with his lovely Amanda by his side, they live to spread the gospel.

Contact the Author

Write to:

Rugged Cross Chapel

Attention: Brandon Emery

502 South Monroe

West Frankfort, IL 62896

CPSIA information can be obtained
at www.ICGtesting.com
Printed in the USA
BVHW030808180520
579803BV00022B/92